# COMMONSENSE METHODS FOR CHILDREN WITH SPECIAL NEEDS:
## Strategies for the Regular Classroom

# Commonsense Methods for Children with Special Needs

Strategies for the Regular Classroom

PETER WESTWOOD

CROOM HELM
London • New York • Sydney

© 1987 Peter Westwood
Croom Helm Ltd, Provident House, Burrell Row,
Beckenham, Kent, BR3 1AT
Croom Helm Australia, 44-50 Waterloo Road,
North Ryde, 2113, New South Wales

Published in the USA by
Croom Helm
in association with Methuen, Inc.
29 West 35th Street
New York, NY 10001

British Library Cataloguing in Publication Data

Westwood, Peter
    Commonsense methods for children with
    special needs: strategies for the regular
    classroom.
    1. Exceptional children — Education
    I. Title
    371.9        LC3965

    ISBN 0-7099-5210-4
    ISBN 0-7099-5247-3

Library of Congress Cataloging in Publication Data

ISBN 0-7099-5210-4
ISBN 0-7099-5247-3

Printed and bound in Great Britain
by Billing & Sons Limited, Worcester.

*c. 1*

# CONTENTS

**Introduction**

**Acknowledgements**

# INTRODUCTION

This book unashamedly sets out to demystify the teaching of children with special needs in regular classes. Hopefully it will build the confidence of regular classroom teachers to tackle the task successfully.

The text is based on the premise that there is very little which is unique or 'special' about the education needed by mildly to moderately handicapped children. It is true that there are a few unusual techniques and approaches which may be needed for example when working with blind or deaf students or those with communication problems; but in general the teaching strategies used with atypical children are not exotic.

We must also acknowledge that children with learning problems, handicaps and disabilities are more like non-handicapped children than they are different from them; and while they may have some special needs their general needs are identical to those of all other children.

Unfortunately, special education is still surrounded by what Meyen, Vergason & Whelan (1972) referred to as 'esoteric mysticism'. This obscures the fact that most so-called special techniques and tricks-of-the-trade are just good basic teaching procedures applied with commonsense and precision. The mystique surrounding special education has regrettably served to make regular classroom teachers feel inadequate when faced with handicapped children. They assume that they lack the necessary knowledge and skills to teach such children. This is largely untrue. *'Special educational needs are not to be regarded as a secret garden into which only the initiated may venture.'* (Thomas: 1986 p.101.)

Throughout this book an effort has been made to deal with children in a non-categorical manner. Much overlap exists in terms of special educational need across all categories of disability and exceptionality. For this reason it is of more practical value to tackle teaching and management in a general way (Reynolds: 1984). Only where it is really relevant is reference made to specific disabilities.

The *Further Reading* section at the end of each chapter provides more detailed coverage of particular handicaps or problems.

*Self-testing exercises* have been presented in each chapter in order to help the reader apply the ideas to his or her own teaching situation.

## Acknowledgements

I wish to thank the following individuals and organisations for permission to quote from or reproduce sections of their work in this book.

The Australian Council for Educational Research for permission to quote from Sophie Bloom's book *'Peer and cross-age tutoring in the school',* published by ACER, Hawthorn, Victoria, 1978.

Merrill Jackson of the Department of Special Education, University of Tasmania, for permission to describe his Visuo-thematic Approach for remedial reading. It is taken from his book *'Reading Disability: experiment, innovation and individual therapy',* published by Angus & Robertson, Sydney.

William McCormick, State Supervisor for Elementary Education, Dover, Delaware, for permission to quote extensively from his article 'Teachers can learn to teach more effectively' in *Educational Leadership,* Vol 37. No 1, 1979.

Ralph Broughton, Head of School of Business and Computing, Adelaide, for permission to use his tests of basic number facts.

Geoff Rogers, Principal, Heathfield Primary School, for permission to reproduce a section of his reading programme *'Truckin' with Kenny'.*

Peter Westwood
Paradise
South Australia.

# 1 HELPING CHILDREN DEVELOP SELF-MANAGEMENT SKILLS

*'. . . children need to be taught self-management skills for planning and carrying out learning experiences with increased independence just as they need to be taught to read.'* (Wang: 1981, p.201)

## Introduction

The term 'self-management' refers to the child's ability to function independently in any given learning environment. In the classroom it relates to such behaviours as knowing how to organise one's materials, knowing what to do when work is completed, knowing how and when to seek help from the teacher or a peer, how to check one's own work for careless errors, how to maintain attention to task without constant supervision or reassurance, how to observe the well established routines in the class such as ordering lunch, having sports equipment or books ready for a specific lesson, knowing when a change of lesson or room is to occur, and so on. The actual self-management skills required by a child will tend to differ slightly from classroom to classroom according to a particular teacher's management style, routines and expectations. For example, in some classrooms a premium is placed upon passive listening, note taking and sustained on-task behaviour, while in other classrooms initiative, group-working skills and co-operation with other children are essential prerequisites for success. The self-management skills required in an 'open education' setting tend to differ from those needed in a more formal or structured setting.

## Self-Management Crucial for Integration

Why are self-management skills important and why have they been given pride of place in the first chapter of this book? The reason is simple: the possession of adequate self-management skills by a handicapped child seems to be one of the most important factors contributing to successful integration of that child in a regular class. In a study comparing successfully integrated mildly retarded children in the upper primary years with similar children who were unsuccessfully integrated in regular classes it was found that the successfully integrated children:

☐ exhibited significantly more initiative and self-management in their classroom behaviour;

1

☐ spent significantly more time usefully engaged upon tasks set by the teacher;
☐ demonstrated significantly better awareness of school rules and routines;
☐ spent significantly less time in inappropriate or disruptive behaviour (Westwood: 1984).

Evidence exists to show that the type of classroom learning environment created by the teacher, and the instructional style used, can both markedly influence the development of self-management and independence in children. Teaching style also determines how effectively classroom learning time is used by the children to increase their skills (Wang & Birch: 1984. Wang & Walberg: 1985).

Some teachers seem to operate with low ability or handicapped children in ways which foster their *dependence* rather than their independence. For example, they may offer too much help and guidance for these children in an attempt to prevent possible difficulties and failures. They may virtually spoon-feed the child using an individual worksheet programme which offers few challenges and calls for no initiative on the child's part. Too much of this type of approach is not what mainstreaming of handicapped children should be about. Not only does it not foster independence, it may well operate in such a way as to segregate the child from the mainstream curriculum and from the peer group for too much of the day.

It could be argued that a child with special needs should only be placed in a regular class when he or she has acquired adequate levels of independence in work habits, self-control, social skills and readiness for basic academic learning. Some of these requisites were identified by Salend (1984) in a review of successful mainstream programmes.

---

*SELF-TESTING EXERCISE 1.1*

*Consider your own class setting (preschool, primary, middle or senior school) and the subjects you cover within the curriculum. Write down a comprehensive list of the knowledge and skills needed by a child to function independently in your setting. The eight examples provided in the first paragraph of this chapter may serve as a starting point.*

---

## Self-Management Can Be Taught

What can be done to teach self-management? Firstly, teachers must believe that such teaching is *important* and that it *is possible* to teach self-management skills to children who lack them. Secondly, teachers need to consider precisely which skills or behaviours are required by their students in order to function independently in their particular classrooms.

## An Example

Usually one would argue that self-managment skills cannot be taught outside the context of situations where they would naturally occur since it would be artificial to do so and there might be no transfer or generalisation if one did. However, experience suggests that there is also some value in teaching particular routines very thoroughly with the whole class in order to be in a position later to refer back to this model when the need arises. An example will be useful here.

### *Teaching students what to do when work is completed*

*Establish attention. Maintain eye contact. Be prepared to call upon specific students for responses, particularly those known to be lacking in self-management and initiative.*

SAY      *'Let's make sure that we all know what we do when we finish a piece of work in this class. Perhaps you finish your maths assignment, or you complete your first draft of a story and you don't need to see me to check it at once. This is what you do.*
*First, you read through the work carefully yourself.'*

WRITE    *on blackboard 'READ YOUR OWN WORK CAREFULLY'.*
*'Why do we do that Allan?' . . . . . .*
*'Good! To check that we have the heading and date and your name. I'll write that on the blackboard.'*

WRITE    *'CHECK HEADING, DATE AND NAME.'*
*Have the class read this aloud in unison.*
*'Good. Any other reasons, Karen?' . . . . . .*
*'Yes, to check for careless mistakes.'*

WRITE    *'CORRECT CARELESS ERRORS.'*
*'Now that you have checked those things you place your work in this tray on my desk. So, what do I write about that on the blackboard?'*

3

*WRITE*    *'PLACE IN Mr. W's TRAY.'*
            *'Good.'*
            *'Then you go back to your desk and you can do one of these things.'*

*WRITE*    *'MOVE ON TO THE NEXT EXERCISE.*
            *COMPLETE ANY UNFINISHED WORK*
            *FROM PREVIOUS LESSON.*
            *FIND A BOOK TO READ SILENTLY OR*
            *TAKE A PUZZLE SHEET.'*

*REVIEW*  *'Let's read those rules through together, then we'll start our handwriting lesson and when you've finished I want you to do exactly what it says on the blackboard without me needing to remind you.'*
            *'Sally' (a girl particularly lacking in self-management), 'come out and point to each one of our rules as we read them together.'*

*(Obviously the routine involved and the language used will be adapted to suit the age and ability of the class.)*

When a child fails to do the correct thing after completing work you are now in a position to refer him or her to the routine previously established.

---

*SELF-TESTING EXERCISE 1.2*

*Write down the steps you might use in teaching any two of the skills listed in Exercise 1.1 as being necessary for independent functioning in your classroom.*

---

**Reinforcement**

In some situations a teacher might employ a 'Star Chart' or other visual recording system to reward at regular intervals all those students who demonstrate the specific self-management skills expected of them. Rewarding would be most frequent immediately after the teaching of the rule (as above, for example), but would not be phased out totally even after several weeks for those who are generally lacking in initiative.

It is important to establish the idea of maintaining the appropriate performance *without prompting*. Remember, when you are constantly reminding the class of what to do you are maintaining the students' dependence. You may need to remind the children with special needs more frequently than the others to begin with and reward more frequently their correct responses; but your long-term aim is to get these children to function independently. When they *do* function independently you have helped them to become more like other childen in the class, . . . *and that is a goal of integration.*


## Locus of Control

The whole issue of self-management and initiative in children, handicapped and non-handicapped, links closely with the personality construct known in psychology as *locus of control.* To explain locus of control one needs to understand that individuals attribute what happens to them in a particular situation either to internal factors (e.g. their own efforts or actions) or to external factors (e.g. luck, chance, things outside their control). The children with an internal locus of control recognise that they can influence events by their own actions, that they do to some extent control their own destiny. Or to bring it down to classroom level, that when they concentrate and try hard they get better results.

The internalisation of locus of control (i.e. the development of responsibility and self-reliance) usually increases rapidly with age if a child experiences normal satisfaction and reinforcement from his or her efforts and responses. However, it has been found that many children with learning problems and with negative school experiences may remain markedly external in their locus of control, feeling that their efforts have little impact on their progress and that what happens to them in learning tasks is unrelated to their own actions (Walden & Ramey: 1983). In its extreme form this externality is usually described as *'learned helplessness'* where the individual anticipates failure immediately any new situation occurs and cannot conceive of being able to change this outcome (Canino: 1981).

The child who remains largely external is likely to be the child who fails to assume normal self-management in class and is prepared to be managed or controlled by 'powerful others' such as the teacher, parent, teacher's aide or more confident peers. There exists a vicious circle wherein the child feels inadequate, is not prepared to take a risk, seems to require support and encouragement, gets it, and develops even more dependence upon others. The teacher's task is one of breaking into this circle and quite deliberately causing the child to recognise the extent to which he or she has control over events and can influence

5

outcomes. It is natural for a teacher to wish to help and support a child with special needs; but it should not be to the extent that all challenge and possibility of failure are totally eliminated. Failure must be possible and children must be helped to see the causal relationship between their own efforts and the outcomes and to accept responsibility for both. Children will become more internal in their locus of control when they really recognise that effort and persistence can overcome failure.

### Strategies for Increasing Internality

Much of the research on matching teaching style or learning environment to a child's perceived or measured locus of control suggests that children who are markedly external respond best at first in a highly structured, predictable, teacher-directed setting, particularly for the learning of basic academic skills. It also suggests that strongly internal students are able to cope well with open or child-centred programmes (Bendell, Tollefson & Fine: 1980). Regardless of this teachers must recognise that for some children with a markedly external locus of control there is a need to help them develop greater internality. This development is likely to be a gradual process, therefore such strategies as suddenly placing external children in a very open, child-centred teaching environment may only increase the number of occasions when they fail and develop an even greater feeling of helplessness and lack of ability. There is a need to work towards the children assuming slightly more responsibility for their work and effort over a period of time. Consideration should be given to the fact that a structured teaching approach which itself does little to increase internality, may be necessary for a while before a child can become independent enough in school work and study to survive in an open situation. For example, a very teacher-directed programme may be needed initially in order to raise the child's level in basic academic skills.

Wang and Stiles (1976) experimented with a system whereby 7 to 8-year-old children were gradually encouraged to plan more and more of their own work (including how long to spend on each task) within the constraints of available classroom resources and time table. Their conclusion was that the self-scheduling system was effective in developing the children's abilities to take increasing responsibility for school learning. It also increased their perceptions of personal responsibility for achievement and success. In other words, the *gradual* increase in the use of self-directed learning may increase self-management skills and internality of locus of control.

6

What are some of the strategies a teacher might use to increase internality? The following list may provide a few clues.

☐ Individual 'contracts' between teacher and child can be introduced in a fairly simple form. These may specify the tasks assigned for a two-hour period or for a morning, but allow the child to decide in what order to tackle the work, how long to spend on each section, and when to seek assistance.

☐ The use of self-instructing material (e.g. programmed kits or computer-assisted instruction) may also help a child to gain an awareness of the extent to which his or her own efforts result in progress and achievement.

☐ Situations may be contrived where children are given a range of graded tasks, some of which will be a little beyond them. When they begin to fail on these tasks they can be shown that with a little more effort on their part and if they seek help when necessary, they can complete the work successfully. The children are taught *how to try* rather than give up.

☐ Teachers who provide only direct correction for school work (i.e. simply marking responses right or wrong without giving feedback and extra practice) are merely establishing a feeling of lack of ability in the child. Feedback to children should be corrective when possible and they should be given the opportunity to prove that they can solve similar items to those that were initially incorrect. Teachers should plan to provide corrective feedback in such daily activities as mental arithmetic or spelling if they want the lower achievers to improve in these areas.

☐ If at some time it is necessary to punish a child for some misdemeanour the punishment should be given immediately following the incident and the child must fully understand the reasons for it. Punishment which is divorced in time and place from the event is likely to exacerbate feelings of helplessness (Canino: 1981). The child should also be given the earliest opportunity to act appropriately in a similar situation and be rewarded for doing so.

☐ While every opportunity should be taken to praise or reward a slower or poorly motivated learner for genuine effort or progress, teachers must avoid rewarding success if no real effort was required. This whole issue of teachers' use of praise merits further discussion.

7

Teachers' use of praise has been well researched, but its overall effects are still somewhat uncertain. It appears to have a differential effect according to the characteristics of the children being praised. Brophy (1979) reviewed studies in this area and concluded that praise does seem important for low ability, anxious, dependent students provided that it is genuine and deserved and the praiseworthy aspects of the performance are specified. A child should know precisely why he or she is being praised if appropriate connections are to be made in the child's mind between effort and outcome. Trivial or redundant praise is very quickly detected by children and serves no useful purpose. Descriptive praise, however, can be extremely helpful. *That's good work, Leeanne. I really like the way you have taken care to keep your letters all the same size.' 'Good, David! Those lines are really straight today because you pressed hard on the ruler.' 'I'm very glad you asked me that question Sara. It shows you are really listening carefully to the story.'*

Thompson, White and Morgan (1982) carried out observations in third grade classrooms and noted that high achieving students received significantly more praise than less able or difficult students. For example they received up to fifty percent more praise than children with behaviour problems. These researchers also made the telling observation that ALL children received far more neutral comment, criticism and warnings than they did praise. They state that teachers were far more disapproving than approving and tended therefore to create negative classroom climate which was not conducive to learning or self-esteem.

## Assessing Locus of Control

Questionnaires exist for the assessment of locus of control in children of various ages (see *Further Reading* section); but it is usually possible to recognise from classroom observation those children with markedly external locus. Teachers should be on the lookout for such children and attempt to intervene to improve the situation.

Lawrence and Winschel (1975) have concluded that retarded children being considered for integration into regular settings should demonstrate a level of internality for both success and failure which is not less than the average level in the regular class. While such a judgement may need to be made rather subjectively, locus of control is certainly one learner characteristic which does need to be taken into account. It may need specific attention once the handicapped child is integrated (Rogers & Saklofske: 1985).

## Summary

This chapter stressed the importance of teaching all children the most effective ways to manage themselves in the regular classroom, to show initiative and to become self-reliant. These attributes are of particular importance in the case of children with handicaps or disabilities since self-management appears to be a crucial prerequisite to successful integration and functioning in the mainstream (Slade: 1986).

Helping children develop self-management skills also involves assisting them to develop a more internal locus of control and to recognise the extent to which their own actions influence their successes and failures. Techniques for fostering this development were discussed.

Everything which has been said in this chapter applies across all categories of handicap and across all ability levels. For example the visually impaired student with above average intelligence needs specific self-management skills quite as much as the sighted child with some degree of hearing loss. Appraisal of each individual's level of self-management should be a starting point for assisting children with special needs to cope more adequately in regular settings.

## Further Reading

Affleck, J., Lowenbraun, S. & Archer, A. (1980) *Teaching the mildly handicapped in the regular classroom (2nd Ed).* Columbus, Merrill.

Brooks, D. M. (1985) The first day at school. *Educational Leadership* 42 (8): 76-78.

Kerr, M. & Nelson, C. M. (1983) *Strategies for managing behaviour problems in the classroom.* Columbus, Merrill.

Little, A. W. (1985) The child's understanding of the causes of academic success and failure. *British Journal of Educational Psychology.* 55: 11-23.

## Locus of Control Questionnaires

Clifford, M. M. (1976) A revised measure of locus of control. *Child Study Journal* 6 (2): 85-90.

Crandall, V.C., Katkovsky, W. & Crandall, V. J. (1965) Intellectual Achievement Responsibility Questionnaire. *Child Development* 36: 91-109.

9

Nowicki, S. & Strickland, B. R. (1973) A locus of control scale for children. *Journal of Consulting and Clinical Psychology* 40 (1): 148-154.

Stephens, M. W. & Delys, P. (1973) A locus of control measure for preschool children. *Developmental Psychology* 9 (1): 55-65.

---

**Application**

*Jason is twelve years old. He has been assessed as moderately intellectually retarded and he spends most of his time at a special school. However, on two mornings each week he attends a regular class in the local school, with some assistance provided in the form of a teacher aide. The intention is that, over a period of time, Jason will be integrated into the regular school on a more permanent basis*

*Jason has difficulty in coping with the demands of the regular school and clearly needs help in adjusting to the routines and expectations there. He is a friendly boy and has no emotional or behavioural problems. His family is very supportive.*

*Consider some of the actions you might take in order to maximise his chances of success when integrated into the regular school.*

---

# 2 THE MANAGEMENT OF DEVIANT BEHAVIOUR

*'Classroom behaviour problems interfere with instruction and with social interactions.'*
(Lewis & Doorlag: 1983, p.114)

## Introduction

Many teachers report that one of their main concerns in the regular classroom is the child who disrupts lessons, seeks too much attention from the teacher or peers and who fails to co-operate when attempts are made to provide extra help or to construct an individualised programme. In other words, the teachers feel that although they may know what the child needs in terms of basic instruction it is impossible to deliver the service because the child is totally unreceptive.

While it is true that some students exhibit behavioural problems in school which are a reflection of stresses or difficulties outside school (e.g. in the family), it is also evident that in some school situations disruptive behaviour and apparent social maladjustment result directly from factors within the learning environment. The student who is bored by work which is trivial and lacks challenge may well become troublesome. The child who is teased or ignored by the peer group may either withdraw or may become attention-seeking or aggressive. The atmosphere in some schools and the approach of some teachers tend to alienate certain students; and therefore maladjustment and the development of poor self-image can be caused by factors within the system rather than within the child.

With younger children the problem of inconsistent management is minimised since most of the curriculum is planned and implemented by one teacher who gets to know the children well. In senior schools many more difficulties can arise.

When cases of disruptive or deviant behaviour are reported, particularly in high schools, it is important to consult with other teachers to discover whether the student is also a problem when in their classes. All teachers who have contact with the maladjusted student will usually need to get together to agree upon a common approach to be used in dealing with the problem behaviour. One of the factors which can add to a maladjusted student's problems in high school is the frequent

11

change of teachers for different subjects. Within the course of one day a student may encounter quite different treatment ranging from the authoritarian to the permissive. This lack of consistency needs to be minimised. It is one of the reasons why some high schools have established 'sub schools' with a smaller but consistent pool of teachers to cater for specific groups of students through in-class support at a more personal level (Lavers, Pickup & Thomson: 1986).

Occasionally of course it is necessary to seek expert advice when a child's deviant behaviour does not respond to consistent forms of management set out below; but in many cases behaviour can be modified successfully within the school setting.

## Changing Behaviour: An Overview

In order to change deviant behaviour in a specific student it is usually necessary to consider all factors which may be supporting the behaviour both directly and indirectly. For example, a girl who openly defies a teacher's request to work quietly on an assignment and not disturb those around her may actually be seeking peer group approval for provoking and standing up to the teacher. She may also be successfully avoiding a situation where she is forced to admit that she cannot do the work which has been set. She may later gain more attention, albeit criticism, from her parents if a letter of complaint is sent home from school. These factors combine to reinforce the status quo. In addition, the girl may be preoccupied with the outcome of some confrontation she had with another teacher in the previous lesson or with another student at lunch time. Finally, if the work appears to her to have no real significance there is little motivation to attempt it. In order to bring about change here the teacher must work to ameliorate the various influences of as many of these factors as possible. This type of global attack on the problem, an attempt to manipulate variables within the total context in which the child operates, has been termed the 'ecological approach' by Hallahan & Kauffman (1986).

A somewhat different approach, but one which is commonly used in conjunction with the ecological for maximum impact is the 'behavioural approach', more often referred to as 'behaviour modification'.

In this approach three assumptions are made:
☐ all behaviour is learned;

☐ behaviour can be changed by altering its consequences;
☐ factors in the environment (in this case the classroom) can be engineered to determine which behaviours will be rewarded and which will be ignored or punished.

Typically a problem behaviour is targeted for change. The factors which are maintaining it are identified. A programme is devised to reshape this behaviour into something more acceptable or more productive through a consistent system of reward, reinforcement or punishment.

Rather emotional criticism is sometimes levelled at behaviour modification programmes. It is suggested that the manipulation of the individual's behaviour and reactions is somehow impersonal and thus out of keeping with humanistic views on the value of interpersonal relationships. However, the precise planning and management of a behaviour modification programme requires very careful observation of how the child, the teacher and other children are interacting with each other and influencing each other's behaviour. Far from being 'impersonal' the techniques used to bring about and maintain change are highly inter-personal.

Some teachers are also deterred from attempting behaviour change programmes because they have been told that very accurate record keeping and charting of frequency and duration of particular behaviours will be required. While data sheets and accurate monitoring of responses are of definite value in clinical settings or where an aide or paraprofessional assistant is available, it is usually unrealistic to expect the busy classroom teacher to maintain such detailed records.

Some examples of behaviour modification techniques will be presented in the following sections of the chapter, together with suggestions for manipulation of the classroom environment to achieve specific results. First it is timely to quote Hallahan and Kauffman's comment to place such strategies in context.

*'Good behaviour management for disturbed children has a lot in common with good behaviour management for all children. The best preventive action any teacher can take is to make sure that the classroom is a happy place where children take pride in their work and learn to treat others with respect.'*
(Hallahan & Kauffman: 1986, p. 184)

13

---

*SELF-TESTING EXERCISE 2.1*

*Identify some problem behaviour which is giving you cause for concern in your present class.*
*Write down as objectively as possible the main features of this behaviour. What are the most obvious characteristics? Why is the behaviour troublesome?*
*Try to identify the specific situations which seem to trigger off the behaviour.*
*What do you do when the behaviour occurs?*
*What do the other children do when the behaviour occurs?*
*Keep this information in mind as you read the remaining sections of this chapter and attempt to select intervention strategies which might be helpful for bringing about the desired changes.*

---

### Identifying the Problem

As previously stated, teachers are often troubled by the child who is constantly seeking attention, interrupting the flow of a lesson and distracting other children. Naturally, many teachers feel threatened by the child who is a constant challenge to their discipline. That feeling of threat causes the situation to get out of hand and the teacher is trapped into confrontations with the child and an on-going war is waged rather than possible solutions sought.

All too often one observes the teacher reacting overtly to undesirable behaviour and at once reinforcing it. Many behaviour problems in the classroom, particularly disruptive and attention-seeking behaviours, have been rewarded by the adult's constant reaction to them. For example, the teacher who spends a lot of time shouting at children or threatening them, is in fact giving them a lot of individual attention at a time when they are behaving in a deviant manner. This is a mis-application of 'social reinforcement' and the teacher unintentionally encourages what he or she is trying to prevent. Some control techniques used by teachers (e.g. public rebuke or physical punishment) can have the effect of strengthening a child's tough self-image and status in the peer group.

If you have a child who is presenting problems to you in terms of control and behaviour it would be useful if you took the necessary time to analyse the possible reasons for this within your classroom setting. These questions may be helpful when attempting to draw up a complete picture of disruptive behaviour.

- ☐ In which lesson is the behaviour least frequent (e.g. the more highly structured sessions or the freer activities)?
- ☐ At what time of day does the behaviour tend to occur (a.m. or p.m.)?
- ☐ What is the noise level like in the room before the problem arises?
- ☐ How is the class organised at the time (groups; individual assignments; etc.)?
- ☐ What am I (the teacher) doing at the time?
- ☐ How is the child in question occupied at the time?
- ☐ What is my immediate response to the behaviour?
- ☐ What is the child's initial reaction to my response?
- ☐ How do the other children respond to the situation?
- ☐ When I have successfully dealt with the problem in the past what strategies have I used?

Notice that the analysis deals with issues which are immediately observable in the classroom. Behaviour analysis does not need to examine the child's past history or search for deep-seated psychological problems as causal explanations for the child's behaviour.

Sometimes changes as simple as restructuring the working groups, reducing noise level in general and closer monitoring of work in progress will significantly reduce the occurrence of the particular behaviour.

## Strategies for Reducing Disruptive Behaviour

### Deliberate ignoring

Ignoring the child can be used far more frequently than most teachers are prepared to accept. If a child begins some form of disruptive behaviour (e.g. calling out to gain attention) the teacher ignores completely that child's response by turning away and giving attention to another student who is responding appropriately. If the peer group can also be taught to ignore a disruptive student and not reinforce the behaviour by acknowledging it and reacting to it, the planned ignoring will be even more successful. This technique is frequently sufficient on its own to modify the behaviour of an intellectually disabled child in a regular class who is merely acting out in ways typical of a younger child.

15

Clearly it is not sufficient merely to ignore disruptive or inappropriate behaviour. It is essential that planned ignoring be combined with a deliberate effort to praise and reinforce that child for appropriate behaviours at other times in the lesson. While it is common to view the frequency of undesirable behaviour in a child as something to reduce, it is more positive to regard the 'non-disruptive' or appropriate behaviours as something to reward and thus increase. It is a useful rule of thumb to be more positive and encouraging than to be critical and negative in your interactions with students.

A teacher cannot ignore extremely disruptive behaviour when there is a danger that someone will be hurt. Nor can a teacher go on ignoring disruptive behaviour if it is putting other children at educational risk through lost learning time. The teacher must intervene to prevent physical danger but should do so quickly, quietly and privately. Private reprimands coupled if necessary with physical restraint, punishment or 'time out' are less likely to bring the inappropriate behaviour to the attention and approval of other children.

## Reinforcement and rewards

In order to modify behaviour, particularly in young or immature children, it may be necessary to introduce a reward system. If social reinforcers like praise, smiles, approval are not effective it will be necessary to determine exactly what things or events *are* rewarding for this child. Reinforcers are very personal and it is necessary to recognise and cater for individual differences. If possible find several reinforcers which may be used to provide variety over a period of time. It may be that the child likes a stamp, a sticker or coloured star, a chance to play a particular game, build a model, construct a puzzle, listen to a taped story on a cassette, or even clean the blackboard! Some teachers use tokens. Tokens are simply a means of providing an immediate and tangible reward. Tokens are usually effective because of their immediacy and students can see them accumulating on the desk as visible evidence of achievement. Tokens can be traded later for back-up reinforcers such as time on a preferred activity, early minutes, a positive report to take home to parents, etc. While not themselves sensitive to individual preferences for particular types of reinforcement, tokens can be exchanged for what is personally reinforcing.

A token chart or star chart may be drawn up for the classroom wall and both individual and group efforts can be rewarded quickly and visibly during the day. Some teachers find the use of a points system helpful in general classroom management; e.g. rewarding the first group ready for work, the group showing high levels of self-management, the children with the highest levels of work output, the individuals working quietly, individuals who exhibit helpful behaviour to others.

Initially we need to reinforce every small step in the right direction but the reinforcement can be reduced over a period of time. Most textbooks on behaviour modification provide some general rules for using reinforcement. It is worth repeating them here.

☐ First, reinforcement must be given immediately after the desired behaviour is shown and must be given at very frequent intervals.

☐ Second, once the desired behaviours are established, reinforcement should be given only at carefully spaced intervals after several correct responses have been made.

☐ Third, the teacher gradually shifts to unpredictable reinforcement so that the newly-acquired behaviour can be sustained for longer and longer periods of time without continued feedback.

---

*SELF-TESTING EXERCISE 2.2*

*Reward systems (points, tokens, stars, privileges, etc.) are frowned upon by some teachers.*
*List the various points for and against the use of such systems to modify behaviour and for general class management.*

---

## Time out

'Time out' refers to the removal of a student completely from a group situation to some other part of the room or even to a separate but safe setting for short periods of isolation. While time out may appear to be directly punishing it is really an extreme form of ignoring. The procedure ensures that the child is not being socially reinforced for misbehaviour.

It is important that every instance of the child's disruptive behaviour should be followed by social isolation if the time out technique is being used. The appropriate behaviour will not be established if at times the inappropriate behaviour is tolerated, at times responded to by punishment and at other times the child is removed from the group. It is essential to be consistent.

Avoid placing a student outside the classroom if in that situation he or she gets other interesting rewards; e.g. being able to peer through the window and attract the attention of other students in the room, making contact with other students in the corridor, watching more interesting events in other parts of the school.

Explosive situations may develop with some disturbed children and a cooling off period will be necessary. A set place should be nominated for this (e.g. a corner of the school library where worksheets may be stored for use by the student). The student will not return to that particular lesson until he or she is in a fit state to be reasoned with and some form of contract can be entered into between teacher and student. The student should, however, be under some form of supervision for all of the time spent out of the classroom.

## Punishment

Punishment, sometimes of the physical kind, is yet another way of eliminating undesirable behaviours. At times punishment is necessary and the consequences do modify behaviour. Punishment, when needed, should be given immediately the deviant behaviour is exhibited. Delayed punishment is virtually useless, particularly with retarded children. Punishment is most effective if it is combined with positive reinforcement. This combination brings about more rapid and effective changes than the use of either procedure alone. The child who pushes or punches other children will learn appropriate behaviour if he or she receives positive reinforcement (praise or tokens) for friendly and co-operative behaviour as well as punishment (loss of privileges, verbal reprimand, time out) for the inappropriate behaviour.

The principal objection to punishment or 'aversive control' is that, while it may temporarily suppress certain behaviours, it may also evoke a variety of undesirable outcomes (fear, a feeling of alienation, resentment, an association between punishment and schooling, a breakdown in the relationship between teacher and student). Punishment may also suppress a child's general responsiveness in a classroom situation as well as eliminating the negative behaviour.

As has been stated previously, punishment should not be used as the sole method for modifying behaviour and controlling certain students. It has as many unfortunate side effects as it has benefits.

## Reducing Aggressive Behaviour

Teachers are bothered most by aggressive behaviour in children (Coleman & Gilliam: 1983). It is therefore worth considering this issue in more detail.

Some of the strategies suggested above for reducing generally disruptive behaviour are applicable also to the reduction of aggression. The following supplementary points, chiefly from Anderson (1978), may be helpful where aggression is the major concern.

Knowing that you have a potentially aggressive child in your class should make you aware of the need to control or limit situations where aggression might be provoked. Too much unstructured time, too many deadspots in lessons, too much unsupervised movement within the room, must be avoided. It may be necessary to give particular thought to the layout of the classroom to allow ease of supervision and access to desks and resources. The establishment of predictable routines and basic rules in the room will help. The teacher, knowing the class well, should be able to anticipate and divert acting-out and aggressive behaviour by a well-timed question, a change of activity or the delegation of a small duty to the problem child.

Other specific strategies include the following:

*Proximity and touch control*

When a child appears to be on the point of losing control move physically closer to him or her, even invading the child's personal space, as a means of reducing or preventing the aggressive action. A touch on the shoulder or a light grasp of the wrist may be all that is needed. The age and maturity of the child are important in deciding how much physical contact is permissible to control potentially volatile situations. The older the student the less appropriate this strategy is likely to be!

*Physical restraint*

If provoked certain children with a low threshold for frustration may lose control so completely that they have to be physically held or removed quickly from the situation to prevent them from hurting themselves or others. This approach should be viewed by the child not as punishment but as a means of saying 'You can't do that'. Some children need to find that they will be controlled when they lose their self-control. In such situations it is vital that the adult does not lose his or her temper but remains calm and neutral.

19

### Provide physical outlets and other alternatives

In educational settings it is important for some children to have extra opportunities for physical exercise and movement in order to 'burn off' excess energy in acceptable ways (e.g. competitive races, circuit training). For certain children this cathartic 'get it out of your system' strategy seems very successful although it can claim no scientific basis at the moment. The present writer found it to be very useful with a special group of secondary students with behaviour problems.

### Teach children to express their anger verbally

Students who are poor communicators, perhaps through language difficulties, often don't know how to handle their own anger and aggression and their reactions are therefore inappropriate. Part of any programme to improve behaviour and reduce the frequency of outbursts should be aimed at helping the student to verbalise the problem. Talking through a threatening situation helps the child to establish control and thus reduces impulsive acting-out behaviour. Accept the child's angry feelings but offer other suggestions for expressing them. For example say *Tell* her you don't like her taking your book'. *Ask* David politely to return your paintbrush'. Then ensure that the child *does* use this approach at once.

### Assertiveness training

Assertiveness training is designed to lead children to understand that they have the right to be themselves and to express their feelings openly. Assertive responses generally are not aggressive responses but they are open and honest. Simply stated, assertive behaviour is being able to express yourself without hurting others.

### Dissolve explosive situation through humour

A joke can help to ease a child out of a temper tantrum or outburst without losing face and can avoid placing teacher and child into confrontation. The joke or humour must not be at the child's expense and must not hint at ridicule or sarcasm.

### Physical punishment

At times physical punishment for a violent outburst may be needed. However, the limited long-term value of this type of punishment was explained earlier in the chapter. It must be recognised that physical punishment for aggressive behaviour is a conflicting reaction since this form of discipline models a violent and aggressive response to a situation. Corporal punishment should be viewed as a very last resort and should certainly not be used repeatedly over a period of time.

Finally, if episodes of aggressive behaviour continue it is essential that the teacher obtain specialist advice via the guidance, counselling or similar support services. Work with the family as well as the child may be indicated.

## Helping Withdrawn or Timid Children

Merrett and Wheldall (1984) have indicated that teachers are much more likely to notice and respond to aggressive and disturbing behaviour than they are to quiet and withdrawn behaviour in the average classroom. The quiet, withdrawn children who cause no problem to the teacher may even be overlooked. They are likely to go unnoticed because their behaviour never disrupts the classroom routine. They annoy no one and they do not constantly come to the teacher's attention.

Teachers are becoming more aware of the significance of extreme shyness and withdrawal as signs of maladjustment. However, as Telford and Sawrey (1981) point out, quiet children are not necessarily emotionally disturbed and may have no problems at all. For example, children reared in families where parents are quiet and reflective are themselves likely to learn similar patterns of behaviour. Reticent and quiet children may be quite happy; and it is a questionable practice to force such children to be assertive.

If a child does have a genuine problem of withdrawal from social interaction with other children the teacher does need to intervene. This may apply particularly to children with physical or intellectual disabilities where social acceptance may be a major problem. Some of the strategies for teaching social skills described in the next chapter will be very important in such cases. Let it suffice here to suggest that the lonely or rejected child may need to be helped to establish a friendship within the class by judicious selection of partners for specific activities (e.g. project work, painting, completion of a puzzle, etc.) and by planning frequent opportunities for the child to experience some very positive outcomes from working with another child. Sometimes the teacher can encourage the child to bring some unusual toy or game from home which can then be shared with another child. Once established even a very tentative friendship must be nurtured by the teacher.

21

Highly formal classrooms where much silent deskwork is expected will do little to foster social development in children lacking these skills. Equally, highly individualised educational programmes for special needs children may attend to their cognitive needs at the expense of their social skills development.

When the social isolation is extreme it may be the result of an almost total lack of social skills, from a history of rejection, from childhood depression, or from some combination of these. Verbal communication may be minimal with such children and even eye-contact may be virtually absent. In many such extreme cases the social isolation may be maintained by negative reinforcement, that is, the behaviour is continued because it avoids unpleasant contact (e.g. ridicule) from other children.

In the literature on socially isolated children it is usually suggested that careful observation be made within the classroom and in the school-yard in order to find the point at which some cautious intervention might be attempted (e.g. getting the child to engage in some parallel play alongside other children as a preliminary step to later joining the play of others, taking a turn, etc.). The teacher will need to guide, support, prompt and reinforce the child through these various stages. In almost all cases the co-operation of the peer group will need to be enlisted if the child is to become an accepted member of that group. Studies have shown that social skills training together with peer group involvement can have lasting effects on improving social adjustment of primary age children.

A number of studies which have focussed upon the integration of handicapped children have indicated that social acceptance of these children into the peer group does not occur spontaneously (Gannon: 1983). Most handicapped children need to be taught how to relate to the non-handicapped children (how to greet them, how to talk with them, how to share, etc.) quite as much as the non-handicapped need to be taught tolerance and understanding of those who are different from themselves.

### Hyperactivity

This form of deviant behaviour, also termed *attention deficit disorder;* is considered to be present in approximately 3% of the school population. The term is often misused and applied to children who are merely bored and restless or who are placed in a class where the teacher lacks good management skills. However there are genuine cases of hyperactivity where the child experiences great difficulty in controlling his or her motor responses and exhibits high levels of inappropriate activity throughout the day. Hyperactivity is also a frequent additional handicap in certain other forms of disability (e.g. cerebral palsy, specific learning disability, retardation due to brain injury).

No single cause for genuine hyperactivity has been identified although the following have all been put forward as possible explanations: central nervous system dysfunction (perhaps due to slow maturation of the motor cortex of the brain), subtle forms of brain damage too slight to be confirmed by neurological testing, allergy to specific substances (e.g. food additives), adverse reactions to environmental stimuli (e.g. fluorescent lighting), inappropriate management of the child at home, maternal alcohol consumption during pregnancy ('Fetal Alcohol Syndrome'). *Most investigators now agree that the hyperactive syndrome encompasses a heterogeneous group of behaviour disorders having different symptom clusters and etiologies'* (Cohen & Minde: 1983).

Hyperactive children usually exhibit below average achievement levels in most school subjects. They may also be poorly co-ordinated. Some have problems with peer relationships. The literature indicates that most hyperactivity diminishes with age even without treatment. However the impaired concentration span and restlessness associated with the condition may well have seriously impeded the child's progress during the important early years of schooling.

Four main approaches are used to treat hyperactivity.

*Pharmacological (the use of medication)*

This is perhaps the most common form of treatment, especially in America. Approximately 80% of hyperactive children do seem to respond positively to drug treatment but the others do not. The main drugs used are Ritalin and Dexedrine. The reduced hyperactivity which accompanies medication does not always result in increased scholastic achievement, perhaps because the child is actually less alert and responsive or because the child is not provided with remedial tuition to help make up the leeway.

Some undesirable side effects have been reported from prolonged use of drugs (slow growth rate, short stature, disturbed sleep patterns).

23

## Nutritional (diet control)

This involves the avoidance of specific foods containing, for example, artificial colourings or preservatives. The Feingold Diet is the best known of these treatments. Its use remains somewhat controversial. Diet control certainly doesn't prove to be effective with all hyperactive children but some parents have claimed that it has been extremely helpful in specific cases.

## Catharsis ('Get it out of your system')

This is merely the application of the strategy described earlier in the chapter whereby children 'burn off' excess energy through outdoor activities at regular intervals.

## Behaviour modification

The hyperactive child's on-task behaviour, attention to work, improved completion rate are all positively reinforced. The overactive behaviour is ignored or punished. In other words the child's classroom behaviour is reshaped to a style which is more acceptable to the teacher and more productive for the child.

Under this approach *cognitive behaviour modification* may also be used. The child is taught to control his or her own responses and behaviour by strategies such as verbal rehearsal or verbal regulation: 'I must work for five minutes on this, then take a break for one minute'. Sometimes video recordings of a child's actions are played back to him or her to focus on and discuss what must be modified. Cognitive behaviour modification is mainly applicable to children of at least average intelligence since they are more able to understand the method and to utilise it consistently.

Owing to the possibility that hyperactivity is caused by different factors in different individuals it is not surprising to find that quite different forms of treatment are advocated and that some work and some do not with particular children.

## Summary

This chapter has presented some specific techniques for controlling and modifying children's troublesome behaviour.

In general a combined ecological-behavioural approach has been advocated whereby a child's problems are not treated in isolation but instead are tackled within the total context of the peer group and the classroom environment.

Particular attention has been devoted to disruptive and aggressive behaviour since this causes the most concern for teachers at all age levels. The problems of hyperactivity have been discussed mainly for the benefit of teachers of young children or of those with specific learning disabilities.

Consideration has also been given to the difficulties encountered by shy, timid or withdrawn children. This latter topic leads to a more detailed coverage of social skills training in the next chapter.

**Further Reading**

Apter, S. J. (1982) *Troubled children: troubled systems.* New York, Pergamon.

Martin, G. & Pear, J. (1978) *Behaviour modification. What it is and how to do it.* Englewood Cliffs, Prentice Hall.

Paul, J. J. & Epanchin, B. C. (1982) *Emotional disturbance in children.* Columbus, Merrill.

Schaefer, C. E. & Millman, H. L. (1981) *How to help children with common problems.* New York, Van Nostrand Reinhold.

Williams, P. (ed.) (1974) *Behaviour problems in school.* London, University of London Press.

*For assessment and reporting purposes see:*

Stott, D. H. (1974) *The Bristol Social Adjustment Guides.* London, Hodder & Stoughton.

*For a very concise and practical guide see:*

Workman, E. A. (1982) *Teaching behavioural self control to students.* Austin, Pro-Ed.

---

**Application**

*Read the following description provided by a teacher when referring a child for assessment by an educational psychologist.*

*"David never seems to be able to keep quiet in my lessons. He always keeps shouting out answers without thinking and he does almost anything to get the attention of other children; shows off almost non-stop. He's on the go all the time. He is a pest before school, too. Before I can get out of my car he is waiting to tell me about*

---

*something that's happened and to carry my bag to the staffroom. He clings on to me when I'm on yard duty and hangs back after school to talk. I sometimes give him jobs to do just to get him out of my hair, but half the time he doesn't finish them. The thing that really annoys me is that he keeps asking me for help during quite simple activities. He doesn't need the help and he stops me from attending to those who do. Then, when I do sit down with another group he deliberately does something to interrupt or to make me cross. He really never gets stuck into his work. He produces very little and I have to virtually stand over him to get him to concentrate. Of course I can't do that all the time. He's really hopeless when we start on something new. He doesn't listen to the instructions so just jumps in and guesses wildly at what has to be done— hit or miss, he doesn't care. Some of the other kids don't like him much because he messes up their team games in the yard. He can't stand losing either! He cheats if he gets the chance. When he's in a group at lunch time I've seen him do really stupid things. The others lead him on and he just does anything to impress them. He's even damaged another teacher's car just because the others dared him to do it."*

What would **you** do to assist a boy like David?

If you have access to the **Bristol Social Adjustment Guides** you could use Form BG1 and transfer this teacher's comments to a more objective type of report. The result would show that David has a form of maladjustment known as **inconsequence.** Check the literature for details of the inconsequential syndrome. (D. H. Stott has described this fully.)

Does the report above tell you anything about the teacher?

# 3 IMPROVING SOCIAL SKILLS AND PEER GROUP ACCEPTANCE

*'Placing handicapped students in the regular classroom is the beginning of an opportunity. But like all opportunities it carries with it the risk of making things worse as well as making things better.'*

(Johnson & Johnson: 1980, p. 10)

## Introduction

The quotation above from Johnson and Johnson (1980) applies most particularly to the issue of social acceptance of a handicapped child when placed in a regular class. The results of most integration studies do not support the belief that integration into the mainstream will spontaneously improve the social status of children with handicaps; in some cases the child's positive social interactions are greatly reduced by such a placement (Gresham: 1984). There are three basic problems:

☐ handicapped children, contrary to popular belief, do not automatically observe and imitate the social models which are around them (Stobart: 1986);

☐ teachers do not tend to intervene positively to promote social interaction on the handicapped child's behalf;

☐ non-handicapped children do not readily demonstrate high levels of acceptance (Gannon: 1983).

At least eight studies indicate that it is common for children with significant speech problems, physical disabilities, retardation, emotional disturbance and poor scholastic achievement to be rejected by their more fortunate peers (Horne: 1982). Admittedly the problems of social acceptance tend to be fewer for the mildly handicapped than for those with more severe and obvious forms of disability (Espiner, Wilton & Glynn: 1985); but even the mildly handicapped may have personality problems, communication difficulties or other characteristics which make it likely that they will be ignored if not openly rejected by the peer group.

Since one of the principal goals of integration is that of enhanced social development for handicapped children it is vitally important that the regular class teacher recognises the need to plan for improvement in this area. Since the late 1970s a great deal has been written concerning social skills training for shy and unforthcoming children and for those with disabilities (see References and *Further Reading* section). Some of these techniques will be discussed in this chapter. At the same time

27

increased attention has also been given in many schools to including 'Social Education' as an identifiable strand within the curriculum. For example, Widlake (1983) quotes the following topics contained within the Scottish Social Education Project, a fairly typical programme of this type.

## SOCIAL EDUCATION

1. *Coming to terms with yourself*
   - *the development of a sense of personal identity*
   - *self-confidence*
   - *personal accountability*

2. *Coming to terms with other people*
   - *the development of tolerance*
   - *the development of adaptability*
   - *the ability to co-operate with others*
   - *an understanding of the nature of authority and the need for social order*

3. *Concern for other people*
   - *the development of sensitivity towards others*
   - *sympathy with others*
   - *the development of a sense of social responsibility.*

In schools where specific attention is given to matters such as these, particularly if issues of disability are openly discussed under section 2 and 3 above, there is a much greater likelihood that differences among individuals will be more readily accepted and that rejection and hostility will be minimised.

Even with these positive advances some teachers still inadvertently deal with children emotionally and physically in ways which contribute to the social exclusion of some class members (Byrnes: 1984). Some examples will illustrate this point.

☐ Teacher A always selects two team-leaders for outdoor games with the instruction to 'choose your own teams'. Guess who is always chosen last or excluded because she is poorly co-ordinated and rather slow? This situation could be totally avoided by the use of a different organisational strategy.

☐ Teacher B always has Wayne sitting near her table so that she can more easily control his behaviour and also provide help when needed. While serving to 'maintain' Wayne in the classroom and attending to two of his educational needs, the approach inevitably isolates the boy from normal interactions with other children during deskwork time. This may not be a problem if he is programmed into group work and pair-activities at other times in the day; but the chances are he may not be.

☐ Teacher C believes that Lynette must have individual work assignments set because she can't cope with the general level of classwork (and this teacher never uses ability or friendship grouping for any purposes). The teacher spends time and effort in programming appropriate material for Lynette and even provides a carrel for her to work in, away from the other children. While this is totally defensible as a method of catering for this child's scholastic needs it must be recognised that it virtually eliminates any social interaction. Is this 'integration'?

☐ Teacher D rarely ventures into the yard unless on duty. If Teacher D spent a little time observing David he would find that this boy is always ignored by other children in the yard at lunch time and at morning break. He spends his time by the door waiting to come back into the classroom (Westwood: 1982).

Obviously some teachers need to be more aware of these situations and also to recognise failures in peer relationships. They must then be prepared to implement suitable strategies which will bring about improvements. These strategies will now be discussed. It must be clear that, although reference is made frequently to children with handicaps or disabilities, the approaches are equally applicable to any child who needs help in personal-social development.

## Identification of Children with Peer Relationship Problems

### Naturalistic observation

The most obvious strategy for identifying children with particular problems is *informal observation* of social interactions within and outside the classroom. A teacher who takes the trouble to note the ways in which children play and work together will quickly identify children who are neglected by their peers or who are openly rejected and become an object of ridicule and teasing. It is very important also to try to observe the surface reasons which appear to give rise to this situation. For example, is the child in question openly obnoxious to others through aggression, hurtful comments, a tendency to spoil games or interfere with work? Or at the other extreme, does the child seem to lack motivation, confidence and skills to initiate contact with others, remaining very much on the outside of any action?

29

Naturalistic observation is probably the most valuable method of identification for the teacher to use since it focuses on the child within the dynamics of peer group interactions and can thus indicate a number of factors which might be modified.

### Sociometric survey

Naturalistic observation tends to identify the most obvious cases of popularity or rejection. It may not pick up some of the subtleties of social interactions in the class. For this reason some teachers find it useful to carry out a whole-class survey in order to get all the children to indicate, in confidence, their main friendship choices. The teacher may interview each child privately or, if the children can write, may give out slips of paper with the numerals 1 to 3 printed on them. The teacher then requests that each child write down first the name of the person he or she would most like to play with or work with as a partner in a classroom activity or at lunchtime. The teacher may then say, 'If that person was away from school who would you choose next?' and that name is listed second. A few teachers might also say, 'If there is anyone in the class you really don't like to work with or play with you can write that person's name against number 3. You don't *have* to write any name there if you get on well with everyone, just leave it blank'. (This last procedure is sometimes criticised by teachers who fear that children may afterwards discuss what they wrote. If handled carefully this problem should not arise.) When the papers are collected the teacher calculates the score for each child on the basis of 2 points for a first choice and 1 point for a second choice. If Susan is chosen three times as the first preference by other children and twice as second preference, her total score is 8 points. The results for each individual in the class can then be tabulated. Some teachers go so far as to map the choices in the form of a sociogram, showing the 'stars' (most popular), the 'isolates' (not chosen by others), mutual pairs and cliques, etc.

The information gained from a sociometric survey may help a teacher to determine the composition of certain working groups in the class. It can sometimes be helpful in identifying which children are named as first preference or second preference by the isolates even though the choice was not reciprocated. There may be a chance to pair these two children for some activities. However, it is often found that isolates merely name the stars in the class and the choice is not realistic or useful. Children who are not chosen or who are listed as 'not liked' should obviously become the target for some of the intervention strategies described in this chapter.

## Rating scales

Gresham (1982) advocates the use of a *peer rating scale* rather than a sociometric survey since he feels that this provides a better measure of 'likeability'. Also it ensures that some children are not forgotten or overlooked as may happen with a sociometric survey of the type described above.

The children are provided with a list of the names of all children in the class and required in confidence to place a score from 1 (not liked very much) to 5 (liked a lot) against each name. Summation of the completed scores will reveal the children who are not liked by most class members as well as showing the level of acceptance of all other children. The result may sometimes correlate highly with naturalistic observation but occasionally quite subtle positive or negative attitudes appear which are not immediately obvious to outside observation (see also Asher & Dodge: 1986).

## Parent nomination

Sometimes a child's social relationship problems at school may be brought to the teacher's attention first by the parent who says 'I'm worried about Paul. He doesn't bring any friends home and doesn't play with other children after school', or 'Marion has been coming home from school saying that the other girls are making fun of her in the yard and on the bus'. This type of information should be followed up by the teacher and treated in a sensitive manner.

---

*SELF-TESTING EXERCISE 3.1*

*Use either the sociometric survey or the rating scale procedure described above with your class.*
*Before charting the results try to predict those children who will obtain low scores.*
*How accurate was your prediction?*
*Did your survey reveal any unexpected information?*
*How might the results of this exercise help you in your day to day work with your class?*

---

## Creating a Supportive Environment

To facilitate social interaction for handicapped children in regular classrooms three conditions are necessary (Finch & Hops: 1983).

☐ The general attitude of the teacher and the peer group needs to be made as positive and accepting as possible.

☐ The environment should be arranged so that the handicapped child has the maximum opportunity to spend time socially involved in group or pair activity, during recess and during academic work in the classroom.

☐ The child needs to be taught the specific skills that may enhance social contact with peers.

### Influencing attitudes

Lack of previous experience with handicapped children and a lack of knowledge about handicapping conditions can lead children (and even teachers) to feel uncomfortable in the presence of a person with a disability. This, in turn, causes them to avoid contact when possible. Where the disabled individual has a marked speech and communication problem, looks grossly abnormal and is poorly co-ordinated the difficulties are greatest. In extreme cases ignorance concerning handicaps can result in damaging prejudice, hostility and rejection.

Fortunately evidence is accumulating to show that attitudes can be significantly changed in teachers and in non-handicapped children. Teachers and peers tend to become more accepting of children with handicaps when they better understand the nature of the disability (Lewis & Doorlag: 1983). Experience has shown that a combination of information about, and direct contact with, handicapped children provides the most powerful positive influence for attitude change.

The following approaches have all been beneficial, particularly when used in combination, in improving attitudes towards handicapped children. Throughout these 'awareness raising' techniques the stress should be upon 'How can we help?' and 'How would we treat someone like that in our class?'

☐ Viewing films or videos depicting disabled children coping well and doing everyday things.

☐ Factual lessons and discussion about particular handicaps.

☐ Having handicapped persons as visitors to the classroom or as guest speakers.

☐ Simulation activities, e.g. simulating deafness, or visual impairment, or being confined to a wheel chair. (Note that unfortunately two conditions which cannot be simulated are intellectual retardation and emotional disturbance. These are also the two which produce the greatest problems in terms of social isolation and rejection in the peer group.)

☐ Reading and discussing stories about handicapped persons and their achievements.

☐ Regular visits as helpers to special schools or centres.

## Creating opportunities

If social learning is to take place it is essential that the socially inept child has the opportunity to be truly involved in all group activities both inside and outside the classroom. If handicapped children are to be socially integrated then group work situations and co-operative learning should be used frequently in pre-school, primary and secondary settings. Unfortunately, while grouping and activity methods are common in the early years of schooling they are less common in the middle school or upper primary school. Even less are they used in the later years when children are faced with a mainly academic curriculum and a fairly rigid timetable.

Much of the work which has supported the value of co-operative learning and grouping within the classroom has been carried out by two brothers, Roger and David Johnson (1980). They make two assumptions: (i) that teachers create classroom environments where competition is not a dominant element; (ii) that teachers use grouping strategies to encourage co-operation among students for at least part of each day. Regrettably both assumptions prove to be false when applied to certain teachers. Some use too much competition among their children on a regular basis. Some teachers make no use at all of grouping. They keep all the children in formal settings working on the same material for the same time regardless of individual differences, actively discouraging any talking or collaboration. The implications here are that if a teacher rarely, if ever, uses grouping as an organisational option, it is unlikely that much will be achieved towards social integration in that classroom.

When utilising group work as an organisational strategy it is important to consider the following points:

☐ Merely establishing groups and setting them to work is not enough. Group members have to be taught how to work together. They must be shown the behaviours which encourage or enable co-operation, e.g. listening to the views of others, sharing, praising one another, offering to help each other. If the task involves the learning of specific content, teach the children how to rehearse and test one another on the material.

☐ Teachers must carefully monitor what is going on during group activities and must intervene when necessary to provide suggestions, encourage the sharing of a task, praise examples of co-operation and teamwork and model co-operative behaviour themselves. Many groups can be helped to function efficiently if the teacher (or the aide or a parent helper) works as a group member without dominating the situation.

☐ The ways in which individual tasks are allotted has to be very carefully planned (division of labour) and the way in which each child can assist another is also made explicit. E.g. 'John, you can help Craig with his writing then he can help you with the lettering for your title board'. Contingent praise for interacting with others should be descriptive. 'Good, John. I can see your friend really appreciates you holding the saw for him.' 'Well done Sue. That's nice of you to help Sharon with that recording.'

☐ The size of the group is also important. Johnson and Johnson suggest a group of two or three members if the children are young or are unskilled in group work. Select the composition of the group carefully to avoid obvious incompatibility. Information from a sociometric survey may help to determine appropriate partners for less popular children.

☐ The choice of topic and tasks for group work is very important. Tasks have to be selected which require collaboration and teamwork. Themes which have proved very successful include: production of a wall display based on a recent visit to a fauna park, planning and rehearsing sketches or skits to be performed, making a video recording, preparing a carnival, sporting activities such as swimming and bowling, co-operative learning of a mathematics assignment (Madden & Slavin: 1983). This latter project (mathematics) involved groups of four or five students, including slower learners, working together to master the set material to a particular standard. The *group result* was evaluated on the basis of how much each individual member had improved on his or her own initial score. The goal structure set for the task clearly involved co-operation. Under this structure, group members have a vested interest in ensuring that other members learn, as the group's success depends on the achievement of all. Helping each other, sharing and tutoring within the group must all be placed at a premium.

It is important to realise that while the short-term results from single projects of this type are beneficial, the effects may not be durable. To ensure maintenance over time any new skills gained must be reinforced constantly and new opportunities created for further interaction.

☐ Talking should be encouraged during group activities. It is interesting to note that subgrouping in the class has the effect of increasing transactional talk (talk specifically directed to another person and requiring a reply) by almost three times the level present under whole-class conditions.

☐ Room arrangement is important. Group members should be in close proximity but still have space to work on materials without getting in each other's way.

☐ Group work must be used frequently enough for the children to learn the skills and routines. Infrequent group work results in children taking too long to settle down.

What other strategies can be used to enhance the handicapped child's chances of positive social integration?

☐ 'Peer tutoring', 'buddy systems' and other helping relationships have all been found effective to a greater or lesser degree; some can result in the development of genuine and lasting friendships.

☐ A greater use of games and play activities of a non-academic type can place the handicapped child in situations where he or she can more easily fit in and work with others.

☐ Make a particular topic (e.g. 'Making friends' or 'Working together') the basis for class discussion. 'If you want someone to play with you at lunchtime what would you say to that person?' 'If you saw someone in the school yard who had just started at the school today how would you greet them? How would you make them feel welcome?' Sometimes teachers prepare follow-up material in the form of worksheets with simple cartoon-type drawings and speech balloons into which the children write the appropriate greetings or comments for the various characters. Much of this can be incorporated into a total social education programme.

☐ It is important to get the peer-group members to reinforce and maintain social interactions with handicapped children. Often they are unaware of the ways in which they can help. They, too, may need to be shown how to initiate contact, how to invite the child with special needs to join in an activity, how to help the child with particular school assignments, etc.

**Social Skills Training**

One of the main reasons why certain handicapped and non-handicapped children are unpopular is that they lack appropriate social skills which might make them more acceptable. They are in a Catch 22 situation since friendless students *ipso facto* have no opportunity to practise social skills and those with poor social skills are unable to form friendships (Lewis & Doorlag: 1983).

Social isolation in childhood may have serious long-term consequences in terms of mental health in adult life so it is vital that isolated and rejected individuals are helped to overcome some of these problems as early as possible. Fortunately there is growing evidence that social behaviours which contribute to positive personal interaction with others can be taught and can have lasting effects (Cartledge & Milburn: 1978).

*What are 'social skills'?*

Broadly speaking social skills are those components of behaviour that are important for persons to initiate, and then maintain, positive interactions with others. The following specific behaviours have been identified as important for social competence.

☐ *Eye contact.* Being able to maintain eye contact with another person to whom you are listening or speaking for at least brief periods of time.

☐ *Facial expression.* Smiling. Showing interest.

☐ *Social distance.* Knowing where to stand relative to others. Knowing when physical contact is inappropriate.

☐ *Quality of voice.* Volume. Pitch. Rate of speech. Clarity. Content.

☐ *Greeting others.* Initiating contact or responding to a greeting. Inviting another child to join you in some activity.

☐ *Making conversation.* Age-appropriate conversational skills. Expressing your feelings. Asking questions. Listening. Showing interest. Responding to questions asked.

☐ *Playing with others and working with others.* Complying with rules. Sharing. Compromising. Helping. Complimenting others. Saying 'Thank you'. Saying you're sorry.

☐ *Gaining attention and/or asking for help.* Using appropriate ways.

☐ *Coping with conflict.* Controlling aggression. Dealing with anger in self and others.

☐ *Grooming and hygiene.*

The above list represents a fairly complex amalgam of non-verbal and verbal skills which all appear crucial for successful social interaction.

As well as having the appropriate social skills an individual also needs *not* to have other behavioural characteristics which prevent easy acceptance by others; e.g. high levels of irritating behaviour (interrupting, poking, shouting, etc.); impulsive and unpredictable reactions; temper tantrums; abusive language; cheating at games. In some cases these undesirable behaviours may need to be eliminated by behaviour modification procedures.

Some writers find it useful to view social skills not as merely 'verbal' or 'non-verbal' but rather as being mainly either *cognitive* or *overt.* Cognitive functions include: *knowing* what to do or not to do by interpreting social cues in a situation (e.g. knowing when an adult is ready to be approached and has time to listen); empathising with or understanding the feelings of others; anticipating the results of your actions. Overt functions include the actual behaviours exhibited: e.g. smiling, gesturing, speaking at an appropriate volume, making eye contact, not standing too close to another person when speaking, etc. Retarded children and those with genuine emotional disturbance tend to have difficulty in acquiring the cognitive functions even after the overt functions have been taught. This is to be expected since the acquisition of these functions (e.g. the concept of what constitutes 'a friend') follows a developmental sequence in all children. Children with special needs will be very much later in reaching a full understanding (Smith: 1982). In some cases the problem has been exacerbated by parents who have overprotected the child and thus reduced social involvement with others.

Attempts have been made to design programmes which will systematically teach any of these skills which are deficient (e.g. The *Catch Project* produced by Cumberland College of Health Sciences, New South Wales, 1983. The *Peers Program* by Hops and associates. See Finch & Hops: 1983). The results from these programmes seem to be very promising. But even without such programmes teachers can assist children to develop social skills.

### How are social skills taught?

In an individual case the first step is obviously to decide where to begin, what the priorities are for this child. Csapo (1983) suggests that teachers should observe and analyse not only what the child does and does not do already, but also determine the specific social skills *needed and valued in that particular age group or class.* It is pointless to teach skills which in that particular context are not immediately functional.

The most meaningful settings in which to enhance a child's social skills are, of course, the classroom and school yard. As suggested in the previous chapter a teacher needs to invervene at times to assist a child to gain entry to a group activity or to work with a carefully chosen partner. The teacher must also praise and reinforce both the target child and the peer group for all instances of co-operative, helpful and friendly behaviour. However, *in situ* intervention is not always feasible, particularly in extreme cases of withdrawal or rejection. At times it may be necessary for a child to be coached thoroughly in a particular skill away from the class situation before that skill can be used in the peer group setting. Franco et al (1983) provide an excellent example of this from a case study of a very shy adolescent. These practitioners focussed on *conversational skills* as being the most important to establish in this youth. In a withdrawal room they worked on four areas: asking questions of others, making reinforcing comments and acknowledging what others say, showing affective warmth, maintaining eye contact. Sessions were held twice weekly for 20 minutes over a fifteen week period. After explanations and demonstrations from a tutor the youth then practised these behaviours with the tutor and applied them in a series of 10-minute conversations with different male and female partners (to aid generalisation). The partners were previously instructed to be warm and friendly but to refrain from asking questions of the subject unless he asked one first. They were also told to keep their responses brief so that the onus would be on the subject to maintain the conversation. The subject was instructed to adapt the strategy of finding out as much as possible about the other person's interests and to keep the conversation going. Observations were made at intervals after the coaching sessions had finished and significant and durable improvements were reported in his classroom interactions.

The *Peers* program (Finch & Hops: 1983) also uses coaching in a withdrawal situation first. The child spends 15 minutes with an adult and one peer in order to establish such basic skills as: how to make friends with others, how to respond to the approaches of others, how to keep interactions going, how to praise others, how to be co-operative. The child is then monitored and rewarded for any evidence of these skills being used during recess time and also during academic work with a partner.

The general training pattern used in most social skills programmes follows these basic steps.

(i) *Definition.* Describe the skill to be taught. Discuss why this particular skill is important and how its use helps interaction to occur. The skill may be illustrated in use in a film-clip, a picture or cartoon, a simulation using puppets, or pointed out to the child by reference to activities going on in the peer group. The teacher may say, 'Watch how she helps him build the wall with the blocks'. 'Look at the two girls sharing the puzzle. Tell me what they are saying to each other.'

(ii) *Model the skill.* Break the skill down into simple components and demonstrate these clearly yourself, or get a selected child to do this.

(iii) *Imitation and rehearsal.* The child tries out the same skill in a structured situation. For this to occur successfully the child must be motivated to perform the skill and must attend carefully and retain what has been demonstrated.

(iv) *Feedback.* This should be informative. 'You've not quite got it yet. You need to look at her while you speak to her. Try it again.' 'That's better! You looked and smiled. Well done.' Feedback via a video recording may be appropriate in some situations.

(v) *Provide opportunity for the skill to be used.* Depending upon the skill just taught small group work or pair activities may be set up to allow the skill to be applied and generalised to the classroom or other natural setting.

(vi) *Intermittent reinforcement.* Watch for instances of the child applying the skill without prompting at other times in the day and later in the week. Provide descriptive praise and reward. Aim for maintenance of the skill once acquired.

To a large extent these behaviours, once established, are likely to be maintained by natural consequences, i.e. by a more satisfying interaction with peers.

---

*SELF-TESTING EXERCISE 3.2*

*Select a social skill from the list provided in this chapter (e.g. 'Working with others' or 'Gaining attention').*
*Plan a series of activities following the six steps above in order to teach and maintain that skill in a child.*

---

## Summary

Many handicapped children encounter problems of peer group acceptance when placed in regular classes. In addition, some non-handicapped children also experience the same difficulties. The ways in which attitudes can be improved, the environment modified to facilitate social interaction and the teaching of specific social skills have been described in this chapter. Evidence suggests that teachers often overlook and therefore neglect this aspect of a child's learning and development in school. Much can be done to assist children with social and personal problems and teachers must recognise their responsibility in this area. To be effective a mainstreaming programme must include provision for enhancing the social acceptance of special needs students (Lewis & Doorlag: 1983).

Poor scholastic achievement seems to be a factor leading to poor social acceptance, even after social skills have been taught. Unless achievement within the curriculum can also be increased acceptance may remain a problem for some children. Attention is therefore focussed on remediation of basic academic skills in the following chapters.

## Further Reading

Canfield, J. & Wells, H. C. (1976) *100 ways to enhance self-concept in the classroom.* Englewood Cliffs, Prentice Hall.

Cartledge, G. & Milburn, J. F. (1980) *Teaching social skills to children.* New York, Pergamon.

Curran, J. P. & Monti, P. M. (1982) *Social skills training.* New York, Guilford.

Gresham, F. M. (1981) Social skills training with handicapped children. *Review of Educational Research* 51 (1): 139-176.

Kafer, N. (1984) The skills of friendship. *SET Research material for teachers.* Hawthorn, Australian Council for Educational Research.

LeCroy, C. W. (ed.) (1983) *Social skills training for children and youth.* New York, Haworth.

Morse, W. C., Ardizzone, J., MacDonald, C. & Pasick, P. (1980) *Affective education for special children and youth.* Reston, Council for Exceptional Children.

Rogers, D. L. & Ross, D. D. (1986) Encouraging positive social interaction among young children. *Young Children* 41 (3): 12-17.

Simpkin, G. I. (1986) The role of language in the social skills curriculum. *Support for Learning* 1 (2): 40-43.

Smith, C. A. (1982) *Promoting the social development of young children.* Palo Alto, Mayfield.

Walker, H. M. et al (1983) *The Walker Social Skills Curriculum.* Austin, Pro-ed.

---

**Application**

□ *Anna is in Year 3 at school and is an extremely shy and timid child. She does not cause any problems in the classroom and her general bookwork is of a good standard. Her teacher has become increasingly concerned that he cannot get Anna to be more forthcoming and assertive both inside and outside the classroom setting. He feels that, if anything, Anna is becoming even more withdrawn. What should he do?*

□ *Many emotionally disturbed children lack the social skills to enable them to relate easily to other children in regular or special classes. A significant number of such children are not only antisocial but also openly aggressive and hostile.*

*Imagine that you have such a child in your class. Describe the steps you might take to modify this child's aggressive behaviour and make him/her more socially acceptable in the group.*

☐ *Some of your colleagues in school suggest that* **social skills** *should be an 'across the curriculum' responsibility and not treated as a separate topic. How do you respond to this suggestion? Is there a place for a social skills curriculum in its own right? How would it be implemented?*

# 4 LITERACY: SOME STARTING POINTS

*'Ideally, a school's reading program should be able to provide reading experiences that result in proficient reading skill for all children, including those who find reading difficult. In practice, schools fall short of this ideal.'*
(Omanson: 1985, p.35)

## Introduction

Learning to read is not a simple task, even for some children of average intelligence (Gillet & Bernard: 1985). It may be a very difficult task indeed for children with significant disabilities such as impaired hearing, cerebral palsy, visual impairment, intellectual retardation or emotional disturbance. For example, *hearing impairment* often limits the child's general vocabulary development and restricts awareness of the phonemic structure of words. *Cerebral palsy,* even if not accompanied by intellectual retardation, may cause visual perceptual problems and a tendency to rapid fatigue in tasks which require carefully controlled eye movements. *Visual impairment* may necessitate the use of magnification aids and enlarged print; or in the case of blindness may require the substitution of braille materials for conventional print. *Intellectual retardation* results in a much slower learning rate; and the child will reach a reading readiness stage at a much later age than is normal. In some cases the child may never reach this stage during the school years if the retardation is moderate to severe. *Emotional disturbance* may cause a child to be so preoccupied that concentration is impossible and motivation is totally lacking. Yet almost all these children can be helped to master at least the basic, if not the higher order reading skills. Quite dramatic improvements can result from special coaching of even the most difficult children.

It has been said that there is no one method, medium, approach or philosophy that holds the key to the process of learning to read. From this it follows that the greater the range and variety of methods known to teachers the more likely it is that they will feel competent to provide appropriate help for slower learners and children with specific learning difficulties.

*'. . . research and our own experience suggests that the approach which is successful with all children with reading difficulties is one which combines features of a number of different approaches and is adapted to a child's individual needs.'* (Gillet & Bernard: 1985, p.16)

## Current Language Arts Philosophy

Remedial teachers may find themselves fighting an up-hill battle with some contemporary reading experts. In the mainstream approach to reading there has been a very strong swing against the teaching of specific component skills such as letter recognition and the sounding and building of words (i.e. a decoding approach). This reaction has come mainly from the field of psycholinguistics (e.g. Smith: 1978). The psycholinguistic approach is based on the premise that from the very earliest stages of reading the learner makes meaning from print by using his or her experience of language to predict words and phrases; indeed, it has been termed a 'psycholinguistic guessing game' by Goodman (see Gollasch: 1982). The emphasis is upon the reader constructing meaning from the sentence or paragraph using all available cues to assist with the process. Three main cueing systems are available:

- ☐ the *semantic* (the meaning of what is being read);
- ☐ the *syntactic* (the logical grammatical structure of the sentences or phrases);
- ☐ the *grapho-phonic* (the correspondence between the symbols in print and the speech-sound values they represent).

The meaning-emphasis viewpoint of the psycholinguistic school implies that if a reader is thinking intelligently about what he or she is reading almost all the 'guessing' is based on semantic and syntactic cues (the 'top-down' approach) and rarely is it necessary to resort to decoding a word from its letters or syllables (the 'bottom-up' approach). For this reason attention to phonics is given low priority.

The views of the psycholinguists may hold true for children who learn to read easily . . . they may well acquire reading skills almost as a natural developmental process. However, teachers who have worked with chronic reading problems know that in the majority of cases it is essential to instruct these children in word recognition, letter knowledge and decoding skills if they are to make progress (Westwood: 1986). In fact, a phonic approach in remedial reading is only contra-indicated if the child has definite auditory perceptual problems or a marked speech articulation defect. Even then, phonic drills are sometimes recommended by a speech therapist as part of a speech training programme.

Problems arise within an exclusively psycholinguistic approach when a child is not at all skilled in contextual

44

guessing. Perhaps the child's experience with language, particularly the more elaborate language of books, has been very restricted and the child's own vocabulary is limited. No teacher would deny that the purpose of reading is to make meaning, or that the more reading one does the more likely one is to become a better reader and to enjoy the activity. However, can one make complete meaning and read fluently without at some stage having acquired the necessary word-attack skills to employ when context clues are inadequate? Stott (1981) is particularly critical of the extent to which the psycholinguists (mainly Frank Smith and Kenneth Goodman) have actively persuaded teachers to minimise their attention to phonic work. 'Phonics' has become an emotive term. In some educational circles the teaching of phonic skills is regarded as reactionary and therefore to be despised . . . an attitude which flies in the face of much recent research which highlights the importance of such instruction (e.g. Lewkowicz: 1980. Ehri & Wilce: 1985. Williams: 1980). Progressive ideas seem to get translated at classroom level into the simplistic belief that 'New is good; old is bad'. In the present case the 'old' is the teaching of phonic decoding skills.

All methods which concentrate from the beginning on reading for meaning leave to chance the learning of the code itself, yet children cannot become independent readers unless they master the code (Naidoo: 1981). Learners differ in the extent to which they pick up phonic principles incidentally. Many children will deduce the code and its rules for themselves but some will not. The judgement of just how much emphasis to give the teaching of phonics needs to be made on an individual basis. As far as gaining an understanding of the grapho-phonic system there seem to be three types of children. Those who gain such insight on their own with little or no direct instruction. Those who need some initial instruction and then make progress on their own. Those who will never master it on their own, they only know as much of the system as they have been taught (Baarda: 1982).

The present writer's experience as a remedial teacher and as a teacher of primary and secondary special classes suggests that the vast majority of children with reading problems exhibit poorly developed phonic knowledge and inefficient word-attack skills. They benefit most from a carefully structured supplementary phonic approach in order to develop the skills which they currently lack. In defence of such teaching Eeds-Kniep (1979) has said, *We do know that this (instruction in*

45

*phonic skills) is something good reading teachers do because they find these techniques helpful and effective when nothing else has been'* (p.916).

It must be stressed here that an *exclusively* phonic approach is not being advocated for any child, with or without special needs. It is being argued that within a total reading programme due attention should be given to the teaching of decoding skills for those children who need this instruction. The psycholinguistic and literature-based programmes emphasise the importance of such matters as:

☐ surrounding the child with stimulating reading material;
☐ creating a climate where reading is an enjoyable, necessary and valued occupation;
☐ the teacher modelling good reading performance and attitude;
☐ giving abundant encouragement to any child who makes the effort to read independently.

These factors create a *necessary but insufficient condition* to ensure that all children will become proficient readers. It is when learning is left to chance that the child with learning problems is at risk.

## The Priority Needs of the Retarded Reader: A Summary

The child who is experiencing difficulties in learning to read needs the following:

☐ An empathic and enthusiastic teacher.
☐ An improved self-image through counselling, success situations, praise, encouragement and recognition of personal progress.
☐ A carefully graded programme, which may mean the making of much supplementary material (worksheets, games, etc.) to use alongside the mainstream programme to provide additional practice. If child-produced or teacher-made books are being used either alongside or instead of a reading scheme they must be used in a structured rather than an informal manner in order to teach effectively.
☐ More time will need to be spent on early reading activities (e.g. flashcards, word-to-picture matching, simple copy-writing, etc.).
☐ More time must be spent in over-learning and reviewing material at each stage (e.g. sentence building, word recognition, etc.).

☐ If a reading scheme is used careful preparation of sight vocabulary is needed before each new book is introduced to ensure success.

☐ Auditory training (e.g. discrimination of sounds, blending sounds into words, segmenting long words into syllables, etc.) may be needed before phonic work is commenced.

☐ Systematic teaching of phonic knowledge and word-building, unless contra-indicated by speech or auditory problems.

☐ Correct letter formation (printing) and handwriting to be taught alongside the reading activities.

☐ Finger-tracing and other multi-sensory approaches (e.g. textured letters) may be needed by a few children to aid assimilation and retention.

☐ Abundant opportunity to read for pleasure and for information.

With these points in mind how does one go about planning appropriate reading instruction for a particular child?

### Diagnostic Assessment

The starting point for any intervention should be based on the results of some form of assessment of the child's current aptitude. Such an assessment need not involve the use of highly sophisticated tests and should not be a lengthy procedure. If a large amount of information is necessary in order to plan a programme the assessment of the child should be spread over several short sessions. One is basically seeking answers to the following four key questions.

---

KEY QUESTIONS

1. What can the child already do without help? What skills has the child developed?

2. What can the child do if given a little prompting and guidance?

3. What gaps exist in the child's previous learning?

4. What skills, concepts or processes are obviously beyond the child's present capabilities and would therefore constitute unreasonable goals in the short-term?

---

Figure 4.1 summarises the key steps involved in implementing a diagnostic approach to an individual learner. It begins with assessment and leads to programme planning and implementation. The procedure is applicable to all the main areas of the curriculum and it will be referred to again in the chapters dealing with writing, spelling and arithmetic.

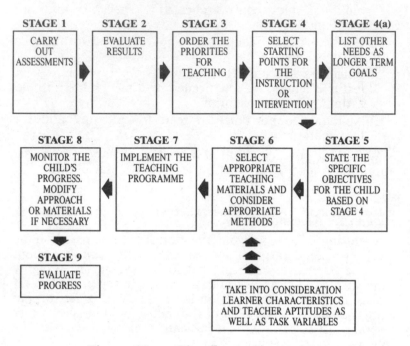

Figure 4.1 — The diagnostic model.

The various stages in Figure 4.1 may be interpreted thus:

**Stage 1** — This may involve the use of checklists, tests, inventories as well as naturalistic observation of the learner.

**Stage 2** — This involves looking at what you have obtained from the assessment of the child performing in a particular skill area (e.g. reading) and applying the four diagnostic key questions referred to above.

**Stage 3** — This involves the identification of the most serious gaps in the child's previous learning which may need to be remedied in order of importance.

**Stages 4 & 5** — These involve (a) the selection of a starting point or teaching aim from the data analysed in Stage 3; and (b) the writing of a specific student performance objective to make that aim operational: e.g. *Teaching aim:* 'to increase the child's basic sight vocabulary'. *Performance objective:* 'Given the twelve most commonly occurring words from the Key Words List presented in random order on flashcards the child will read these aloud without hesitation or prompting'.

**Stage 6** — This involves (a) the selection of appropriate materials (books, kits, apparatus, etc.) to assist in working towards the stated objective; and (b) consideration of the most appropriate method of working with this child, based on a knowledge of his or her characteristics (e.g. learning style, interests, concentration span, etc.) and your own personal competencies in dealing with small group or individual tuition.

**Stage 7** — This involves implementing the teaching programme with the child for a period of sufficient duration and frequency to have some impact on progress.

**Stage 8** — This involves an overlap with Stage 7 in that you are required to determine whether your programme is working effectively by the use of on-going (formative) evaluation of the child's performance.

**Stage 9** — This involves some definite procedure for assessing how much real change has occurred in the child as a result of the programme (summative evaluation). This is usually carried out at the end of the teaching block and is linked directly with the stated objectives at Stage 5.

Note that when working with and testing a child it is important to observe the child's learning style and *task-approach skills* as well as the actual responses being given. For example, has the child selected a particular answer after careful thought or was it an impulsive guess? Is the child hesitant and under-achieving because he or she is wary of the adult and unwilling to take a risk?

Diagnosis must eventually involve a consideration of the total situation in which the learner operates. As well as learner characteristics it is important to evaluate also the *learning task* itself (e.g. level of difficulty, its relevance to the child's interests, etc.), the *teaching method* being used, the *physical environment* in which the child is being taught and the quality of the

49

*relationship* between the child and the teacher and the child and the peer group. In other words, educational failure (and therefore the means by which to change the status quo) is rarely only due to factors within the child. Failure usually stems from a complex interaction among all the variables just listed.

Diagnostic approaches are referred to as either *formal* or *informal*. The term formal diagnosis usually implies that published tests (e.g. reading attainment tests or reading diagnostic tests) are used in order to obtain specific information about a learner's current status in certain selected areas such as comprehension, word recognition, phonic knowledge. Sometimes particular component skills are assessed such as auditory discrimination, visual discrimination, short-term auditory memory or sound blending. Formal assessment may be carried out for a whole class simultaneously, for example by the use of pencil-and-paper group testing. At other times formal assessment must involve the careful and detailed testing of one child alone using standardised or criterion referenced tests. Formal assessment of this type is useful in indicating where current achievement stops and new learning needs to begin. It is usually supplemented by information from informal testing.

Informal diagnosis involves such procedures as direct observation of learners in action and an examination of what they actually do or what they produce during a lesson. Informal assessment in reading includes, for example, listening to the child read aloud from an appropriate book and detecting the presence or absence of particular strategies for word attack, use of context, prediction, comprehension, general fluency and expression. The use of teacher-made *informal reading inventories* may be of value here. The inventories comprise graded samples (paragraphs) from books available in the classroom. A child's level of success on the inventory will provide a good indication of the readability level of books he or she can cope with independently and for instructional purposes. Performance on the inventory will also indicate the child's general approach to the task of reading, (e.g. hasty and careless, hesitant and unwilling to risk a guess, etc.). The books by Mercer (1985) and Bader (1980) listed in the *Further Reading* section contain much useful information concerning the design of informal reading inventories. These authors suggest that accuracy in reading the graded passages should be 95% if the material is to be read independently by the child and 90% for material to be used for instructional purposes. Material with an error rate of 15% or more is considered to be at frustration level (too difficult).

While a child is reading from a book or an inventory the teacher should attempt to discover any persistent error patterns which emerge. The child's ability to self-correct is also worth noting.

---

*SELF-TESTING EXERCISE 4.1*

*Prepare an informal reading inventory using photocopied passages from appropriate books in your classroom. The material should be carefully graded, beginning at the level of very simple vocabulary and short sentences embedded in passages approximately 50 words in length. Extend this to more complex and demanding material in 150-200 word samples. Prepare six passages and use the inventory with a selected child. Evaluate the results in detail, indicating what the child can and cannot do in terms of word recognition, use of context, etc.*

---

*Assessing the non-reader*

If an individual, regardless of age, appears to be a non-reader it is worth obtaining the following information:

☐ Can the learner concentrate upon a learning task and listen to the teacher, or is he or she too distractible and hyperactive?

☐ Has the learner adequate language experience and sufficient vocabulary development to begin reading?

☐ Does the learner seem able to grasp that words have unit values in print, that the spaces between words have some significance?

☐ Does the learner have the concepts of 'letter' and 'word'? Does the learner have an awareness of the left-to-right progression in a printed sentence?

☐ Is the learner capable of carrying out visual discrimination of pictures, of letters and of words? Can he/she correctly perform matching exercises?

☐ Does the learner recognise *any* words by sight? (E.g. own name; environmental signs such as 'CLOSED' or 'KEEP OUT'.)

☐ Can the learner complete picture-to-word matching activities correctly after a brief period of instruction?

☐ Can the learner carry out a simple learning task involving sight recognition of two words taught from flashcards without picture clues (e.g. 'MY' and 'BOOK')?

☐ Can the learner co-ordinate hand and eye sufficiently to copy simple geometric shapes and basic letter shapes? It may be useful to ask a child to draw a person, a house and a tree to gain some impression of the child's concepts of, and ability to reproduce, these familiar objects. The following set of shapes can be presented on separate cards approximately 12cm by 10cm for the child to copy. The ages below each figure indicate the age by which most children can copy the shape correctly.

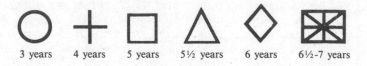

| ⚪ | ✚ | ⬜ | △ | ◇ | ❇ |
|---|---|---|---|---|---|
| 3 years | 4 years | 5 years | 5½ years | 6 years | 6½-7 years |

Hand and eye co-ordination has been overrated in the past as an important prerequisite for *reading*. Many children whose ability to copy shapes or join dot-to-dot patterns is poor are still capable of learning to read. Poor co-ordination is more important as a problem in the development of writing skills.

☐ Has the learner developed adequate listening skills to attend to the subtleties of speech sounds within words? This is more important if the early approach to reading is going to stress phonic aspects and sound blending.

☐ Does the child know the names or the sounds of any letters when these are presented in printed form?

---

*SELF-TESTING EXERCISE 4.2*

*Prepare a set of materials and accompanying activities which will enable you to carry out these readiness assessments covered in the ten questions above.*

---

### Evaluating the retarded reader

For the child who is not a complete non-reader and has at least some functional skills the following areas are worthy of assessment.

☐ *Basic sight vocabulary.* What can the child already do in terms of instant recognition of the most commonly occurring words in print? The *Dolch Vocabulary List,* the *Key Words to Literacy List* or the material provided in the book *Reading Rescue* (Gillet & Bernard: 1985) all provide appropriate material for this area of assessment.

☐ *Miscues and use of context.* When the child is reading aloud from age-appropriate material what types of error are made? Do the words conform to the meaning of the sentence or are they totally out of keeping with the message? Does the child tend to self-correct when errors are made in order to restore meaning?

☐ *Word-attack skills.* When reading aloud does the child attempt to sound-out and build an unfamiliar word even without being instructed to do so? If not, can the child do this when he or she is encouraged to try? Has the child developed a fully functional set of phonic principles? In particular, does the child know all the common single letter sounds, digraphs, blends, prefixes and suffixes? Can the child divide a regular but lengthy word into its component syllables?

**N.B.** It is often most helpful to devise word lists using nonsense words rather than real words in order to isolate and assess a child's particular word-attack skills. For example, the ability to sound and blend consonant-vowel-consonant words is easily evaluated using such invented words as V-O-B, L-U-T, D-E-P, rather than C-A-T, V-A-N, S-I-T, since these real words may be known by sight. Similar but more demanding nonsense lists can be invented to cover digraphs, blends, etc. (e.g TR-A-SP CH-O-ST).

☐ *Auditory skills.* Can the child *discriminate* between similar but not identical speech sounds when these are presented orally in word-pairs (e.g. MOUSE—MOUTH, CAT—CAP, MONEY—MONKEY). Teachers can devise their own word lists for this purpose; or use can be made of *Wepman's Auditory Discrimination Test* or that contained in McLeod's *Domain Phonic Survey.*

Can the child *analyse or segment* familiar words into their component sounds? This is a listening and oral test, not a reading test. If the child hears the word 'REMEM-BER' can he or she break this into the units RE-MEM-BER? If testing this you must first give some practice so that the child understands what is required.

Can the child *blend or synthesise* sounds in order to pronounce a given word (e.g. CR I-SP). Again, this is a listening test and not a reading test; the child does not see the word in print. The following diagnostic test designed by David Moseley* is very useful for assessment of this skill.

**Instructions:**

*Say 'I am going to say some words very slowly so that you can hear each letter sound. I want you to tell me what the word is. If I say O-N you say ON'.*

*Discontinue after five consecutive failures.*

*Sound the phonemes at rate of about one each second.*

**The words:**

| | | | |
|---|---|---|---|
| *i - t* | *l - o - t* | *f-r-o-g* | *s-p-e-n-d* |
| *n - o* | *m - a - n* | *w-i-n-k* | *c-r-i-s-p* |
| *w - e* | *r - e - d* | *c-o-l-d* | *p-l-a-n-t* |
| *d - o* | *c - u - p* | *b-u-m-p* | *f-r-o-s-t* |
| *a - m* | *b - i - g* | *r-e-s-t* | *t-r-u-n-k* |

**Scoring:** $1 + \dfrac{\textbf{\underline{total number correct}}}{5}$ *(e.g. $1 + \dfrac{15}{5} = 4$)*

**Interpretation:**

| Child's Age | Normal Score | Extreme Difficulty |
|---|---|---|
| *6 - 7* | *3 to 4* | *2 or less* |
| *7 - 8* | *4 to 5* | *2 or less* |
| *8 - 9* | *4 to 5* | *2 or less* |
| *9 - 10* | *4 to 5* | *3 or less* |
| *10 - 11* | *5* | *3 or less* |

Auditory discrimination, auditory analysis and sound blending have all been recognised as extremely important subskills for progress in reading (Fox & Routh: 1984). Limited short-term auditory memory span has also been identified as a possible cause of difficulty in sound blending and word building since the child cannot retain the complete set of sounds long enough to synthesise the word. Poor short-term memory may also disrupt comprehension (Turner & Alston: 1986). A standard procedure for assessment of short-term auditory memory is given below from Westwood (1975).

☐ *Auditory short-term memory.* The learner is presented orally with digits from Set 1. If he/she repeats these correctly the next group of digits from Set 1 is given. If the child fails to repeat a group correctly a group of the same length is taken from Set 2. If this is also failed a

*(*D. V. Moseley. Centre for Learning Disabilities, N.S.M.H.C., London. Reproduced with permission.)*

group of the same length is taken from Set 3. Thus *three attempts* at each level of difficulty is permitted. The following age levels indicate the point at which most children of that age can succeed with at least one correct repetition out of three trials.

By chronological age

| | |
|---|---|
| 3 years | 2 digits |
| 4 years | 3 digits |
| 5 years | 4 digits |
| 6/7 years | 5 digits |
| 8/9 years | 6 digits |
| 10/11 + years | 7 digits |

In applying this test one is looking for failure below 4 digits since this will suggest probable difficulties in word-building at other than a very simple level. If a child has a marked deficiency in memory span it will have a bearing on the teaching strategies to be selected. It may be a deficiency which cannot be corrected and may need to be bypassed, for example by avoiding undue emphasis upon single letter phonic decoding but rather teaching syllable attack from the start. Specific improvement in short-term memory may not result from memory training activities (Chase, Lyon & Ericsson: 1981).

### The Test:

Present the sequence without rhythm at one digit per ½ second.

| Set 1 | Set 2 | Set 3 |
|---|---|---|
| 7 | 4 | 2 |
| 3-5 | 5-7 | 4-9 |
| 6-1-9 | 2-8-1 | 3-7-4 |
| 4-2-8-3 | 6-4-3-9 | 5-8-2-7 |
| 5-4-7-9-2 | 8-1-9-5-7 | 4-1-8-7-3 |
| 8-3-5-2-7-1 | 5-3-7-6-2-4 | 9-1-6-5-2-8 |
| 5-7-1-9-2-4-8 | 9-2-8-4-7-1-6 | 7-3-1-8-2-9-6 |

☐ *Comprehension.* Reading can hardly be called true reading unless children are understanding what they are reading about, therefore evaluation of this aspect of performance is crucial. Informal questions can be asked after a child has read a passage silently or aloud. The questions should not be solely at a factual-recall level (literal comprehension), e.g. 'How old is the girl in the story?' 'What is the boy's name?', but should probe for understanding at higher levels of inference and critical interpretation.

(E.g. 'Why did the man react in that way? Was he angry or shocked?' 'When the lady suggested they look for the goods in another shop was she being helpful or rude?' 'What do *you* think of the suggestion the leader of the team makes?')

Exercises using *cloze procedure* are sometimes useful in both testing and developing comprehension and contextual cueing. A passage of some 100 to 150 words is selected and every fifth or sixth word (approximately) is deleted leaving a gap. Can the child read the passage and provide a word in each case which conforms to the meaning of the passage and to the grammatical structure of the sentence?

---

*SELF-TESTING EXERCISE 4.3*

*Prepare appropriate materials for assessment in the areas indicated above, paying particular attention to sight vocabulary, word-attack skills and comprehension.*

*While teacher-made materials are very acceptable for this type of assessment you may also find the following tests useful.*

**The Standard Reading Tests.** *(Daniels & Diack. Publisher: Chatto & Windus, London.)*

**Neale's Analysis of Reading Ability.** *(Neale. Publisher: Macmillan, London.)*

**Gap** *and* **Gapadol Reading Tests.** *(McLeod & Anderson. Publisher: Heinemann, Melbourne.)*

**Gates-McKillop Reading Diagnostic Tests.** *(Gates & McKillop. Publisher: Teachers College Press, New York.)*

**Domain Phonic Test.** *(McLeod & Atkinson. Publisher: Oliver & Boyd, Edinburgh.)*

**Co-operative Reading Comprehension Test.** *(Publisher: Australian Council for Educational Research, Hawthorn.)*

---

*Assessing the child who has reached a reading plateau*

Some children appear to reach a temporary plateau in their reading development at or about a reading age of 8½ years to 9 years. Many of the assessment techniques covered in the previous section may help to uncover the possible areas of difficulty in these children; but attention must also be given to the following three factors.

□ *Error Analysis.* It is with children who have reached a reading plateau that error analysis can be extremely valuable in pinpointing specific gaps in the child's current reading skills. Possibly the child has not yet mastered certain letter clusters as phonic sight habits and will either make random guesses or will refuse or mispronounce unfamiliar words containing these letter clusters.

To employ the error analysis procedure it is usual to listen to the child read aloud on several different occasions using material which is reasonably challenging but not at frustration level. As each error is made the teacher provides a quick correction for the child to maintain continuity. The performance is recorded on tape for later analysis. Different reading specialists have suggested different categories into which errors may be analysed (e.g. Neale: 1966. Goodman & Burke: 1972. Kemp: 1980). The present writer has developed the table below after several years of experimentation.

| | |
|---|---|
| Faulty vowel | |
| Faulty consonant | |
| Faulty digraphs and blends | |
| Reversal | |
| Sounds added | |
| Sounds omitted | |
| Refusal | |
| Words added | |
| Words omitted | |
| Contextual guess | |
| Unidentified | |

If the error does not destroy the meaning of the sentence it is classified as a 'contextual guess' and has no particular diagnostic significance. If, however, the word is totally out of context or is mispronounced after the child has attempted to decode it phonetically, the actual nature of the error or errors within the word should be considered. Basically, the teacher is asking 'What is it in the original word that the child has failed to recognise or has rendered incorrectly?'

☐ *Readability of text*. Consider the difficulty level of the material the child is attempting to read. Has he or she selected books which are at frustration level? Reading skills will not advance if the child is faced constantly with text which is too difficult.

☐ *Affective factors*. With a child who has ceased to make progress it is vitally important to consider affective as well as cognitive factors. For example, has the child developed a very negative, 'couldn't-care-less' attitude towards reading and avoids the task whenever possible? Does the child experience any enjoyment from reading? Is the material in the book in keeping with the child's real interests? Is the working relationship between the child and the teacher (or tutor) a positive one? Is there any incentive to improve? Where difficulties are detected in these areas it is just as important to attempt to change matters if possible as it is to concentrate merely on the skills aspect of reading development.

## Summary

All the procedures described in Chapter 4 for the assessment of a child who is retarded in reading are applicable to children with very varied forms of physical, sensory or intellectual disability. A particular disability does not require a specific and unique form of diagnostic evaluation; one is simply attempting to find out with some degree of precision what the child can and cannot do at the present time in this skill area. It may well be that the child with the more severe form of handicap, or with multiple handicaps, will be assessed in readiness-type skills typical of a much younger child, but the actual procedure involved in assessment does not differ.

According to how the child performs on the initial diagnostic assessment a teacher would either focus on the *early or pre-reading skills* (e.g. visual discrimination, word-to-picture matching, letter knowledge, etc.), on *intermediate skills* such as word-attack, contextual cueing, etc., or *higher order reading skills* such as syllabification, prediction, and literal, interpretive or critical levels of comprehension. Activities will then be programmed to assist the child to develop beyond the present stage. Programme planning will be described in detail in the next chapter, together with a description of a number of methods which may be employed to assist children with reading difficulties, regardless of the cause of such difficulties. Most of these methods can be used within the regular classroom and do not require the children to be withdrawn for remedial assistance.

## Further Reading

Bader, L. (1980) *Reading diagnosis and remediation in classroom and clinic.* New York, Macmillan.

Bradley, L. (1985) *Assessing reading difficulties (2nd ed).* London, Macmillan.

Ekwall, E. E. (1977) *Locating and correcting reading difficulties.* Columbus, Merrill.

Gillet, S. & Bernard, M. (1985) *Reading rescue.* Hawthorn, A.C.E.R.

Groff, P. (1986) The maturing of phonics instruction. *The Reading Teacher* 39 (9): 919-923.

Mercer, C. D. & Mercer, A. R. (1985) *Teaching students with learning problems (2nd ed).* Columbus, Merrill.

Pikulski, J. J. & Shanahan, T. (1982) *Approaches to the informal evaluation of reading.* Newark, International Reading Assn.

Westwood, P. S. (1975) *The remedial teacher's handbook.* Edinburgh, Oliver & Boyd.

### Application

*Imagine that you are appointed to a school where no systematic check is made of children's reading standards at any age level.*

*You are asked by the head teacher to devise some appropriate system for assessing the overall reading standards in the school and for identifying those children in need of special assistance.*

*After considerable time and effort you plan what seems to be a viable set of procedures and you present your plans at a staff meeting.*

*Much to your surprise several of your colleagues object very strongly to your suggestions, stating that they do not believe in testing children in any formal way. They say that tests don't tell them anything they don't already know. They also imply that testing makes children anxious; and when parents get to know their children's results this can cause a great deal of unnecessary concern in some cases.*

*What are you going to do?*

*One obvious action would be to withdraw your plan and give in to your colleagues' arguments. However, you feel quite strongly that some monitoring of standards is necessary and you are prepared to argue your case.*

*Try to summarise the points you would make to support your suggested programme. Try also to answer the specific objections raised by your colleagues.*

*In general, how might the regular assessment of reading throughout the school influence the achievement levels of individual children?*

# 5 PROGRAMMING FOR READING: METHODS AND MATERIALS

*'. . . early classroom methods should take account of the ten to fifteen percent of children in the class who risk "dyslexic" problems. They need to be taught what the others intuitively discover before they are hopelessly confused and demoralised.'* (Yule: 1986, p.83)

## Introduction

Following the careful assessment of a learner's aptitudes as suggested in the previous chapter it should be possible to plan the appropriate starting points for intervention. The following case study will help to introduce this topic of programme planning, moving on from informal and formal test results to classroom action.

## CASE STUDY: David

*Chronological age at time of testing, 8 years 6 months.*

**Reading Level.** *Reading Age 7.2 years.*

**Verbal Intelligence.** *I.Q. 114 (WISC-R).*

**Vocabulary Level.** *Vocabulary equivalent to that of an average nine year-old (Crichton Scale).*

**Basic Sight Vocabulary.** *David has a very good grasp of the first 150 words on the 'Key Words List' with the following exceptions:*

*off   of   for   (all confused)*

*what   where   were   when   with   (all confused)*

*right   (not known at all)*

**Phonic Skills.**

*(i) All common single letters known.*

*(ii) Knows most of the common digraphs and blends by sight, but some uncertainty with sp sk st str spr. More difficulty evident with endings, especially __ng __nd __nk __tion.*

*(iii) Auditory discrimination perfect (Domain Test).*

*(iv) Phoneme blending perfect (Moseley's Test).*

*(v) Short-term auditory memory (Digit Span Test) normal for age.*

61

*Points (iii) to (v) indicate that there is absolutely no reason why David should not continue to make progress with a predominantly phonic approach.*

**Word-building Skills.** *These are very poor. He lacks any systematic approach to unfamiliar words (Schonell Test R5).*

**Spelling Ability.** *Spelling age 6.8 years (Daniels & Diack Test 11). This is slightly below his reading age but not markedly so.*

**CONCLUSIONS.** *David is typical of the child who has all the necessary subskills to make good progress in reading, particularly with the decoding of unfamiliar words, but* **fails to make use of his phonic knowledge** *to any great extent preferring to cling to a 'look-and-guess' technique. His reading errors reveal that he very frequently guesses at new words from a quick glance at the first letter with some vague help from the context. He makes little or no use of the information provided by the middle and ending of the word.*

*It should be noted that David is of at least average intelligence and is not deficient in oral language skills. At the present time his reading level is roughly one year behind his own age level. While this is not a very serious difference now it may well become so if no special tuition is provided.*

*He is reading* **Flamingo Book 3** *which is just appropriate for his reading level. However, it contains too few phonemically regular words for him to experience much success in sounding and building words not already known by sight.*

**RECOMMENDATIONS.** *Supplement his present scheme with extra work to develop word-study technique. It may be that a few other children in the class will benefit from such help and they could work as a small group for the following activities.*

*(a) Select a short story or passage at a suitable instructional level. Have the child (children) read the first paragraph through silently. Now ask each child in turn to read aloud three or four sentences. When an error is made or the child hesitates you, the teacher, must model the most efficient way of tackling that word. Indicate that guessing from the first letter is not*

*effective. 'How do we use the middle and end of the word to help us decode it? Can we break the word into syllables? Does the word now make sense?'*

*Continue with the reading aloud and repeat the modelling whenever necessary. Give praise and encouragement for any evidence of David applying your technique for word-attack without prompting.*

*This activity will need to be carried out for roughly ten minutes each day.*

(b) *Worksheets or workcards with exercises requiring the child to supply the correct middle vowel, syllable or ending will help to focus attention on the skill which David needs to develop. This type of exercise should not be used too much since it is divorced from reading for meaning.*

(c) *The* **Brickwall Game II** *and some of the* **Snake Games** *from Stott's* **Programmed Reading Kit** *would fit in well at this stage of word building.*

(d) *David takes his book home already each evening, could he also take home a few words to learn to read and spell? Perhaps five words grouped according to visual or phonemic similarity would be helpful here, for example words illustrating the silent* **e** *rule or the* **ar** *unit (car, far, tar, bar, park) etc.*

(e) *I would certainly make some use of phonic dictation with this boy, not as a* **testing** *procedure but to train him to listen carefully to the temporal order of sounds within words, particularly ending sounds. The material taken home to learn might form the basis for this dictation.*

(f) *Alongside the* **Flamingo** *books use* **The Lookout Gang** *series (Gibson) and the 'C' level books from the* **Ladybird Scheme** *from book 5C onwards. The school already has the series* **Sounds for Reading** *(Nisbet) and you may find suitable material for word study in the* **Teacher's Guidebook** *at level three. Several of the* **Remedial Refresher Cards** *(Gibson) would be useful for work assignments, provided some teaching had preceded each unit.*

*Above all else it is important that David devotes time to reading each day. At the moment it is far from being his favourite subject and one needs to get him more interested in reading for pleasure. He is likely*

> *to need a great deal of praise and encouragement as well as extra attention if his motivation is to improve. It is important that you have a serious chat with his parents to ensure that they do not put undue pressure on him at home in the area of reading but that they are made aware of ways they **can help** to supplement your work with him at school.*

Hopefully, the type of report presented above helps the teacher to identify David's instructional needs fairly accurately. After a suitable period of time David's progress should be evaluated carefully and it may well be that the supplementary teaching can be phased out if he has overcome his weaknesses. If not, some modification to his present programme will be needed.

Of course not all children will be at David's particular level and attention will now be given to approaches suitable for absolute beginners in reading. Later in the chapter methods for more advanced readers than David are presented.

## Pre- and Early Reading Experiences

For most children a carefully structured pre-reading programme is unnecessary. Once the child has adjusted to the demands of school life, instruction in reading can and should begin. For a few, *particularly those with significant retardation or perceptual difficulties,* it will be valuable to provide pre-reading experiences which prepare these children for beginning reading and take them to the threshold of simple word recognition. Training in listening skills, encouraging a liking for stories, ensuring familiarity with language patterns, all form important parts of the programme. Indeed, aural-oral language enrichment activities form the basis of all reading readiness programmes (Sippola: 1985. Williams: 1986).

When the pre-reading activities involve word-to-word matching, word-to-picture matching and letter and word copying, the child is ready to enter the next stage of development. The golden rule to remember in remedial teaching is to make the work link as closely as possible with the educational skills and media the child is needing to use at this time. For instance, in pre-reading activities, if the child needs to improve in visual discrimination it is likely to be of maximum benefit if letter and word matching are utilised rather than the matching of pictures and geometrical shapes.

64

## Form perception and visual discrimination

If oral language is adequate and if the child has realised that the marks on paper represent words which can be spoken, the next important skill to consider is that of form perception which, at its highest level, is reflected in the fine discrimination of letters and letter sequences.

If a young or disabled child is very poor at form perception the teaching will need to begin with the fitting of hardboard shapes into inset formboards, matching and sorting simple regular shapes and feeling these shapes hidden within a puzzle box where the child can handle but *not see* them. He or she then identifies the shape just handled from a set of line drawings outside the box. Later the activity can be reintroduced using small plastic letters of the alphabet in the puzzle box, these being handled and identified in the same way. This activity is useful for holding attention through active participation and enjoyment.

Other useful activities which will help to develop awareness of shape and form and encourage attention to detail include: copying regular shapes using drinking straws, drawing around templates, drawing within stencils, tracing figures, completing unfinished figures on worksheets. These activities are of particular importance to young children with impaired vision or with perceptual problems.

The sequence for training visual discrimination should follow the progression:

1. Picture matching ⟶ 2. Shape matching ⟶ 3. Letter-like shape matching ⟶ 4. Letter and word matching.

The point of entry for a particular child into this sequence will be determined from diagnostic assessment.

**N.B.** If a child is able to sort and match word shapes and has adequate language development, he or she is ready to read through one of the various whole-word approaches even though phonic readiness may not be present. The child will benefit from a language-experience or shared-book approach (see later).

## Visual retention and visual sequential memory

It is helpful for some children to be trained in the careful observation of material which they are then required to reproduce from memory in correct sequential order. This is often done using picture cards (for example, cow, house, man, ball, cup), but it is more useful if the material provides letter sequences; for example

Sometimes the training requires the child to *write* the sequence after brief exposure on a flashcard. This aids early spelling skills as well as word recognition skills for reading.

### Hand-eye co-ordination and motor control

Building, cutting, sticking, threading, tracing, jigsaw making and games activities which go on in all preschool and junior classrooms are already developing fine motor co-ordination for most children. A few will need much longer at such tasks and may benefit from specific training. Large chalkboard work using big movements is a very useful starting point. In cases of very poor control it is helpful if the teacher guides the child's hand in order to make the movements smooth and rhythmical and to establish a correct motor pattern. Simple mazes and dot-to-dot patterns produced as worksheets are a useful extension from large scale movements to finer control. Writing patterns can be used for both chalkboard work and practice sheets. It is vital that children who do have some degree of difficulty in co-ordination are taught correct letter formation. Handwriting or printing should not be left to incidental learning. This applies particularly to children with cerebral palsy, spina bifida, hydrocephalus or with neurological dysfunction resulting in clumsiness.

Problems of laterality (that is, choice of hand for manual tasks and dominant eye in visual tasks) and poor directional sense (orientation) are frequently found to be present in slow learners and children with specific learning difficulties. These factors are rarely the cause of a child's learning problems but rather another symptom of inefficient functioning. Some American programmes stress the need to establish a strong lateral preference in a child before attempting remediation in academic skills and they suggest exercises for doing this. However, such programmes have not proved to be particularly successful; and most teachers today would not deliberately set out to rectify crossed-laterality or to alter hand preferences in their children with special needs.

Crossed-laterality, lack of firmly established lateral preference and poor directional sense frequently result in a marked tendency to *reverse* shapes (e.g. letters or words in reading, numerals in arithmetic). In extreme cases mirror-writing may be produced by the child. It is quite normal for children up to the age of about six-and-a-half years to confuse letters like **p, b, d** and **q** in their reading and writing, so undue attention to this problem would be out of place below that age. However, reversal problems which continue in some cases through to the secondary school level do require attention. A few ideas for remediation are provided here.

If a child above the age of seven years is still confusing **p, b, d, q** or **u, n,** it is essential that he or she should be given a motor cue (kinaesthetic training) to establish the correct direction of these letters. Finger-tracing one of the letters until mastered is probably the most positive way to overcome the problem. First the child should close eyes or wear a blindfold while the teacher guides the index finger of his or her preferred hand over the shape of the letter 'b' on the blackboard. The letter is simultaneously sounded or named as the tracing is repeated several times. The teacher now takes the child's finger over a series of other letters and the child must indicate quickly and clearly, but still with eyes closed, each time a letter 'b' is traced. The aim here is basically to give a child a physical image against which to discriminate **d** and **b**. As soon as the child has mastered one of the letters thoroughly the *'Post-box Game'* from Stott's *Programmed Reading Kit* (1962) can be used, together with a self-help card showing that the 'little **b**' is really

only the bottom half of capital **B.** This card can be left displayed in the classroom for some time after training. It is important to stress that if the child is given a correct motor-cue for letter and numeral formation in the early stages of handwriting instruction many of the reversal problems would not persist.

If the child's balance and general co-ordination are very poor teachers may need to plan specific activities for inclusion in a daily P.E. programme (e.g. hopping, beam walking, small ball catching, etc.). In some schools these children may be receiving special physical education or therapy from a visiting teacher and close liaison with this teacher will be essential if the activities are to be integrated and reinforced in the regular class programme.

67

## Auditory training

It has been shown conclusively (Treiman: 1985) that in the process of learning to read auditory skills rapidly become just as important as oral language skill and visual skills. Progress beyond the stage of building up a basic sight vocabulary using whole-word recognition is dependent upon the development of phonic skills. As previously stated the acquisition of phonic skill is in turn dependent upon adequate auditory discrimination auditory analysis, auditory blending and short-term auditory memory. It is likely that these processes are also involved to some extent in spelling ability.

Auditory training need not always precede any introduction to reading unless a child's auditory perception is markedly deficient (e.g. where a child has a known hearing loss and auditory training is recommended as part of a programme to increase the child's use of residual hearing). Usually auditory training can be provided *alongside* the child's early reading experiences while a basic sight vocabulary is being built up. Many of the activities which are being used to teach basic phonic knowledge are also simultaneously training listening skills. For instance, many of the games from the *Programmed Reading Kit* (Stott: 1962) are developing auditory discrimination, auditory analysis and auditory blending as well as teaching the sound values of the particular symbols involved in the game.

The principal aims of auditory training are to increase awareness of sound patterns, to encourage careful attention to speech sounds and to develop the skills of listening. Brief consideration will be given to the four auditory processes referred to above.

*Auditory discrimination.* A teacher will find it useful to collect pictures from mailorder catalogues and colour supplements to use in games requiring auditory discrimination. The pictures may be set out in pairs and the child must quickly touch one of a pair of pictures when the word is called: for example, 'pear' (pictures show 'bear' and 'pear'), 'Three' (pictures show 'three' and 'tree'). Worksheets can also be made with pictures of objects which the child must identify when the initial sound is given. The *Domain Phonic Workshop* (McLeod & Atkinson: 1972) contains similar sheets already prepared. When games like these have been played it is useful to get the child to say the name of each pictured object clearly and then to listen to his or her own voice played back on a tape recorder, thus dealing with articulation alongside auditory discrimination.

Classroom games which involve 'Finding the odd one out' (for example, boy, bone, bag, hand, band) and may involve rhyme (for example, sand, hand, feet, land, band) are popular. With young children 'I spy' games using initial letter sounds rather than letter names are useful.

*Auditory analysis.* Some of the activities listed above have included simple levels of auditory analysis . . . isolating the initial letter sound. Games can be extended to listening for final sounds (for example, 'Put a line under the pictures that end like snake'. Pictures show rake, bucket, cake, ball).

Auditory analysis can be taught, or at least encouraged, by spending a little time in taking words apart into their component sounds, raising the actual process to the level of awareness in the child. For example, 'What's this picture, Jackie? Yes. Good. It's a frog. Let's listen to that word FROG. Let's say it very slowly. FR-O-G. You try it'. This involves listening, not reading.

*Auditory blending.* This is also referred to as sound blending or phoneme blending and is the complementary process to auditory analysis. Encourage the children to gain experience in putting speech sounds together to build a word. 'I spy with my little eye a picture of a FR-O-G'. Use the same technique while reading or telling a story to the children. 'The boy came to the wall. He couldn't get over. The door was st-u-ck . . .' Children quickly supply the words as the story goes on. Sound blending is also helped in the early stages of word-building from print with simple consonant-vowel-consonant words (l-o-t; m-a-n). Teachers must be on the lookout for children who find this process difficult since it is a vital subskill for reading and can be trained if necessary.

*Short-term auditory memory.* Here one is on much more shaky ground. It is questionable whether this function can be improved by specific training. Certainly some poor short-term retention is due to *lack of attention;* and any strategies which improve and develop careful listening are likely to influence short-term retention of auditory material. Some experts recommend getting the children to repeat sentences (simple messages, for example) deliberately making them a little longer over a period of time. The learning of simple rhymes and jingles may also help. Extending the earlier listening games involving blending of words to include now multisyllabic items may also be useful to increase immediate memory span for sounds (EX-ER-CISE, MULT-I-PLY, AS-TRO-NAUT, GE-O-GRAPH-IC-AL).

69

Drills involving repetition of strings of digits are unlikely to have any value whatsoever.

It is necessary to identify children with extremely limited immediate memory span so that a different approach is developed for them when word-attack skills are taught.

## Intervention: Selecting a Reading Method

Assuming that the learner has the necessary entry skills of adequate visual discrimination and at least some ability to converse in simple sentences, two complementary approaches might be used, *Shared-book experience* and *Language-experience reading*. The two approaches are entirely compatible with modern theories of language acquisition and reading skill development. In both cases when used for remedial teaching purposes they require a much greater degree of structuring than is necessary when applied to children with no learning problems. Neither method precludes the teaching of word-attack skills as will be illustrated in the descriptions below.

### *Shared-book Experience* (Holdaway: 1982)

In the shared-book approach children are brought to an enjoyment of reading first through stories read by the teacher using a large size, specially prepared book which can be seen easily by the group or class of children. Holdaway says that the book should have the same visual impact from 20 feet away as a normal book would have on the knee of the child. Stories, poems, jingles and songs which children love and which present an opportunity for them to join in, provide excellent material for the early stages. Familiarity with the language patterns involved in the stories is developed and reinforced in a natural way. Attention (on-task behaviour) is easily maintained by the teacher who can present the material with enthusiasm and whole-hearted enjoyment. The pages of the book become a giant teaching-aid on which the teacher can develop word recognition and letter recognition skills informally, as well as convey the story. The teacher may, for example, place a hand over a word (or mask it in some other way) so that the group of children must suggest what the word is likely to be, thus helping them to develop an awareness of contextual cues and language patterns.

As a beginning-reading method the approach has proved equal to or superior to other methods and produces very positive attitudes towards reading, even in the slower children.

With the least able children it is likely that, in order to establish greater independence, more attention will need to be devoted to mastering letter sounds; but this too can be done enjoyably through games, rhymes and songs rather than 'drills'. For example, the *Pictogram System* (Wendon: 1983) developed by a very imaginative teacher in England, uses alliteration in the names of the key characters to help the children associate and remember a sound with a symbol. This approach could easily be integrated into the shared-book programme. The pictograms themselves are letters with pictures superimposed in such a way that they reinforce the shape of the letter while creating a story link in the child's mind. The **h** is presented as the **H**airy **H**atman who walks along in words whispering **h, h, h,** for **h**hairy **h**hat. The **w** is introduced as the **W**icked **W**ater **W**itch, with her two pools of water held within the shape of the letter. More complex combinations are all covered in the scheme. For example when **a** (for apple) is next to **w** (for Water Witch) the witch casts a spell which makes the apple taste **aw**ful.

Games and activities from Stott's *Programmed Reading Kit* could also be used to provide a carefully structured and sequenced progression for the acquisition of phonic skills; not instead of, but in addition to the small group or whole class shared-book experience.

## Language-experience approach

The language-experience approach basically uses the child's own language to produce carefully controlled amounts of reading material. It could be described as a form of 'dictated story' approach. From the viewpoint of the slow-learner or failing reader the approach combines two major advantages. There is the possibility of utilising the child's own interests to generate material for reading and writing, and the teacher is able to work within the child's current level of language competence at all times. Moyle (1982) has stressed the tremendous value of this approach for children who are well below average in general language development. The work produced is usually relevant and motivating. Where does one begin with this approach?

With the young child or the child of very limited ability the starting point for the language-experience approach can be the labelling by the teacher or aide of some of the child's art work or drawings, no matter how primitive, with captions which the child suggests. *'This is my cat, Dotty'*, *'I can ride my BMX bike fast'*. The child and teacher together read these captions and revise them for a few minutes each day, without at this stage drawing attention to individual letters or words. If *Breakthrough to Literacy* materials are available in the classroom the child can be encouraged to build these sentences using word-cards in a sentence holder. During this early stage of the programme the child can be helped to contribute a dictated sentence following some class excursion to the airport or a farm. *'I saw a Jumbo Jet', 'The cow licked David on the face.'* These sentences are added, along with others from the class, to the picture-map which the class has produced as part of the follow-up to the excursion. Again, they are not in any way analysed or drilled, and serve the purpose of establishing in the learner's mind the notion that 'What I say can be written down'.

After a few weeks of this introductory work the child is ready to make his or her first book. A topic is carefully selected: e.g. 'Speedway'. The teacher or child produces some visual material which will provide the illustration for the first page, perhaps a picture of the child's favourite speedway rider from a magazine. Teacher and child talk about the rider and from the discussion they agree upon *one* brief statement which can be written under the picture: *'This is Chris Copley.'* The teacher writes (prints) the agreed statement for the child who then copies it carefully under the teacher's version. If the child cannot copy due to perceptual-motor or co-ordination problems, he or she can trace over the words with a coloured pencil or wax crayon. Both teacher and child then read the statement together once or twice and the child is left to paste the picture carefully into the book. Even this activity must be closely supervised with some children in order that the page looks attractive rather than messy. With some older children they can be encouraged to type the same sentence on a sheet of paper and paste that into the book to help generalisation from handwritten to typed form of the same words.

Next day the child is presented with the same statement written on a strip of card: **This is Chris Copley.** Without reference to the book the child is encouraged to read the words. He or she may have forgotten the material so some brief revision is needed. The child then cuts the strip of card into separate word cards. These are placed at random on the desk and the child has to arrange them in correct sequence. If the child fails he or she must spend time matching the word cards against the original in the book until the sequencing task can be performed correctly. At this point the teacher picks up one of the cards, perhaps the word 'is', and using it as a small flashcard asks the child to pronounce the word. This is continued until the child can recognise each word out of context. The word cards are then placed in an envelope stapled in the back cover of the book ready to be revised the following day.

Over the next week the child continues to produce a page of his or her book with much guidance from an adult. Revision of the previous day's words ensures repetition and overlearning to the point of mastery. The teacher's control of what is written will ensure that not too much is added to the book each day which might result in failure to master the new words. If the child is allowed to dictate too much material this will result in failure to learn and loss of satisfaction.

Once important sight words are mastered these can be checked off or coloured in on a vocabulary list in the front cover of the child's book. McNally and Murray's *Key Words to Literacy List* or the Dolch sight vocabulary lists are very appropriate for this purpose. Such charting of progress in the book gives the child visual evidence of improvement and also indicates to the teacher what has been covered so far and what still needs to be taught. If certain words seem to present particular problems for the child games and activities can be introduced to repeat and overlearn these words until mastered (e.g. Word Bingo). Gradually the amount written can be increased and after some months a child will need less and less direct help in constructing his or her own sentences. The approach may sound slow and tedious but it does result in even the most resistant cases of reading failure making progress. It is highly structured and the growth in word recognition skills is cumulative.

At some stage in the programme the teacher must help the child to expand his or her word-attack skills. For example, perhaps the child has used the word 'crash' in writing about the speedway interest. In a separate booklet the teacher can help the child to learn the value of the blend 'cr' by collecting other cr words (crab, crook, cross, cry, etc.). Similarly they can experiment with the unit 'ash' from the word 'crash' (b-ash; d-ash; c-ash; r-ash; etc.). This incidental word study linked with meaningful material from the child's own book is important, but it will be inadequate for developing fully functional decoding skills. It will be necessary to use some sequential material such as Stott's Kit to supplement this.

Once a child has made a good start using this language-experience approach he or she can be introduced to an appropriate book from a reading scheme or supplementary series. It is wise to prepare the way for this transition by including in the child's final language-experience book most of the words which will be met in this first book in the scheme.

The basic principles of the language-experience approach can be used with non-literate adults and those learning English as a second language.

Clearly the shared-book experience can operate in parallel with the individualised language-experience approach in both whole-class and remedial group situations.

### The Visuo-thematic approach (Jackson: 1972)

Jackson described a carefully structured variation of the language-experience approach which he had found useful in clinical settings. He has called the approach 'visuo-thematic'. The learner (child or adult) is presented with a visual stimulus picture which has a number of ideas in it to generate discussion and to suggest a story without too much imagination being required. Jackson found detailed cartoons from magazines or newspapers to be useful and he suggests that the learner be encouraged to seek out suitable material to bring to each session. Jackson outlines the procedure in the following steps.

The child obtains a picture which he or she pastes on a piece of cardboard, together with a matchbox in the corner. This matchbox is to house small cards containing all the words the child can think of to describe various aspects of the picture. The child is then required to have three columns ruled on a page headed, respectively, *naming words, describing words, action words.* He or she is then asked to try to think of at least six words which can be placed in each of the above columns, thus giving a total of at least 18 words for the picture. The words are written out at home or during the lesson in their appropriate columns and the child is then asked to put each word on a small card and place it in the box. In this way a 'library' of pictures and their associated vocabularies is built up by the child. When the child comes to the lesson the teacher or aide checks the words for accuracy and tests the child's ability to recall them. Some practice is then given in spelling the words.

The next step is for the child to construct his or her own series of questions about aspects of the picture. The child is then asked to write a story about the picture and to select a title. The story is read by the child together with the adult and any corrections noted. After this the child is asked to re-write

74

the story or type it in its final form and to paste it in the book beside the vocabulary lists. This procedure is repeated at least once a week, using on each occasion a different story but the same format and structure.

## The use of comic strips (Johnson & Johnson: 1977)

Johnson and Johnson have described a most successful and motivating beginning-reading approach for primary or very slow learning secondary students. They recommend the use of children's comic strips, adopting the following procedure.

The children select a comic strip. They number each individual picture in logical sequence. They cut and paste each picture in the top half of a blank sheet of A4 paper. They then dictate their own perception of the 'story' to the teacher or other tutor (e.g. parent, peer, aide). The teacher prints the words for each story below the appropriate pictures, reading these back to the child and then asking the child to read them unaided. Finally the pages are secured together and a cover is made. The children can then share their small booklets with others in the class. The story dictated by a child does not have to be identical with the one intended by the artist. The teacher can accept the children's own versions.

Johnson and Johnson point out that during the process of writing down the child's dictated story the teacher can draw attention to certain single letters and letter groups in order to begin to develop some basic word-attack skills. Words which are particularly difficult but important are put on flashcards for revision and practice. At a later stage the child copies the story into his own book. Gradually the child will be able to construct more of the story without adult help.

Another possible use of comic strips and cartoons for remedial reading and writing involves the removal of the captions or the 'speech-balloons' using some form of correcting fluid or white ink. The child then discusses with the teacher what the characters might be saying and is helped to write the words into the 'speech-balloons'. These are then read to the teacher and to other children.

## Audio-visual approaches

Of the various approaches which use audio-visual presentation there is one which is particularly motivating for older students, *The Bowmar Reading Incentive Program*. This presents reasonably sophisticated themes like drag racing, motor cycles, hot-air balloons, etc., through the use of film strip, sound commentary on tape and a student's reading book which embodies the same language as presented in the taped commentary. The range of kits in this series each have a teacher's guidebook and sets of the student books. The very colourful and lively presentation, and the opportunity for the student to become familiar with the language structure and vocabulary associated with each theme before having to read it in the books, are the principal attractions. The use of the taped commentary in conjunction with the books then allows for abundant repetition and over-learning *(Bowmar Reading Incentive Program.* Radlauer & Radlauer: 1974).

Teachers can, of course, make their own programmes for use with a tape recorder. Indeed, this item of hardware is an indispensable aid in all remedial situations. It may be used for nothing more ambitious than pre-recording of popular stories which the children can listen to through headsets while following the text in the book. In this way material which would otherwise be at frustration level for a child can be presented in a very meaningful manner. Other uses of the tape may be to programme aspects of phonic work or spelling assignments, or to set comprehension questions at literal, interpretive, critical and creative levels.

The use of popular songs provides repetition with enjoyment and has proved to be useful in remedial or special class situations. A zig-zag book containing the words from a current song is prepared for the child or the small group. The children follow the words in the book as the song is played from a cassette. Later the words are read without the music and some key words may be put on to flashcards to be recognised out of context.

*Micro-computers and word-processors* can be used to help a child develop word recognition, decoding and sentence completion skills. They also present the opportunity for the teacher to devise specific teaching programmes to improve comprehension skills.

The *overhead-projector* is also valuable for presenting aspects of reading in a predominantly visual way. Many teachers make their own transparencies and use colour to good advantage in developing word study skills. The Milliken Publishing Company has produced an excellent programme *Look, Listen and Learn.* The material comprises attractive O.H.P. transparencies and a parallel set of spirit duplicating master-sheets to allow for the printing of assignments for individual or class use. The quality of this material is extremely good and probably surpasses anything which a teacher could produce.

The *Languagemaster* (Bell & Howell) remains a very popular machine for use in remedial settings. Its main value lies in the fact that the child is actively engaged in the operation of the machine and is using visual, vocal, and auditory channels simultaneously (and is also receiving immediate corrective feedback).

The machine is in essence a tape-player and recorder that allows the simultaneous presentation of moving visual material with auditory output (or oral input from the learner). A card, with a strip of recording tape at its base, is fed into the machine in a right-to-left direction (the child therefore scans it in a left-to-right direction). The card contains space for words and/or pictures to be presented and the tape gives the auditory information relating to the words or pictures. By switching to a different track the child can record his or her response to the question and can play back this answer for checking with the original.

The *Languagemaster* has had a long history of useful service in remedial and special classes. As well as being useful for teaching and overlearning of the basic sight vocabulary it can be used to reinforce the learning of new words in a reading scheme or in the child's language-experience book. It can also be used to teach a child certain 'self-help' skills within the reading process. For example, key words or particularly difficult vocabulary from a specific book can be put on to the Languagemaster cards, together with the recording of the word. The child reads the page in the book, guessing the difficult word, then plays the card to check or learn the pronunciation.

## The Cloze technique

Cloze technique is a simple approach designed to make a reader more aware of context cues and meaning as aids to guessing unfamiliar words. The procedure merely requires that certain words in a sentence or paragraph be deleted and the reader is asked to read the paragraph and supply the possible words which might fill the gaps.

E.g. *It was Monday morning and Leanne should have been going to sch____. She was still in ____. She was hot and her throat was ____.*
*'I think I had better send for the d____,' said her _____. 'No school for you ____.'*

77

These activities can involve group work. The prepared paragraphs are duplicated on sheets for the children or displayed on the overhead projector. As a group the children discuss the best alternatives and then present these to the teacher. Reading, vocabulary and comprehension are all being developed by a closer attention to logical sentence structure and meaning.

Variations on the cloze technique involve leaving the initial letter or letters of the deleted word to provide a clue; or at the other extreme, deleting several consecutive words, thus requiring the student to provide a phrase which might be appropriate. The use of the cloze procedure can be integrated as part of the shared-book experiences already described.

### The Impress Method (also known as the 'Neurological Impress Method' and the 'Read-Along Approach')

The Impress reading method is a unison reading procedure in which the student and the teacher read aloud simultaneously at a natural rate. The student is permitted to use the index finger to keep the place on the page, and may even be physically guided to do so by the teacher.

The Impress Method is particularly useful when a child has developed some word recognition skill but is lacking in fluency and expression. It is recommended that sessions should last roughly fifteen minutes and be provided on a very regular basis for several months. It may be necessary to repeat the same sentences or paragraphs several times until the student becomes fluent at reading the material alone.

The Impress Method is very appropriate for use in peer-tutoring situations where one child who is a better reader provides assistance for a less able friend. In such cases the 'tutor' usually needs to be shown how to act effectively as a helper (see Chapter 8).

### Rebus Reading Approaches

Any approach which uses a picture or symbol in place of a particular word may be described as a 'rebus' approach. The method allows a child to feel that he or she is reading at a functional level through by-passing the difficult nouns for the time being. A simple illustration of this principle is presented below from a series called *Truckin' with Kenny,* written by Geoff Rogers when working as a support teacher.

78

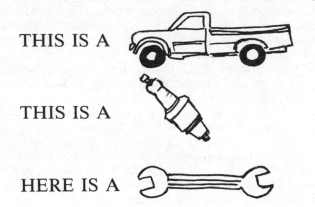

THIS IS A

THIS IS A

HERE IS A

It is an approach which can serve to boost confidence in the early stages of a remedial programme and can allow a story-line to be developed without the tight constraints of vocabulary control.

### Multisensory or multimodal approaches

The names Fernald, Gillingham, Stillman and Orton usually come to mind when multisensory approaches are mentioned. Basically all of these educators have advocated methods which use as many channels of input to the learner as possible. The methods usually involve the learner finger-tracing over the letter-shape or word-shape to be mastered while at the same time saying and hearing the auditory component and seeing the visual component.

The Fernald approach involves four stages.

☐ First the learner selects a particular word which he or she wants to learn. The teacher writes the word in blackboard-size writing (cursive) on a card. The child then finger-traces the word, saying each syllable as it is traced. This is repeated until the learner feels capable of writing the word from memory. As new words are mastered they are filed away in a card index for later revision. As soon as the learner knows a few words these are used for constructing simple sentences.

☐ The second stage involves the elimination of direct finger-tracing and the child is encouraged to learn the words through studying their visual appearance and then writing

79

them from memory. This stage improves visual imagery and may thus be used also for remedial instruction in the correct spelling of irregular words. The words are still stored on card and used for frequent revision. The material is usually consolidated through the child producing his or her own small books.

☐ The third stage continues to develop visual word-study techniques and encourages a more rapid memorisation of the words followed by swift writing. The word-card drill is usually retained only for particular words which give difficulty. At this stage the child also begins to attempt to read new material prepared by the teacher.

☐ The final stage involves the child becoming almost entirely independent in his or her reading skill, having generalised an understanding of word structure and having been helped to make use of context cues.

The Gillingham and Stillman Approach and the Orton Approach are basically the same as the Fernald Approach, employing a Visual-Auditory-Kinaesthetic-Tactile (VAKT) method. The only significant difference is the emphasis given to sounding-out rather than slowly pronouncing the word during the finger-tracing stages. More attention is given to learning the letter sounds and applying these in word-attack.

It can be argued that multisensory approaches using several channels of input simultaneously help a child to integrate, at a neurological level, what is seen with what is heard, whether it be a letter or a word. On the other hand VAKT approaches may well succeed where other methods have failed because they cause the learner to focus more intently on the learning task. Whatever the reason, this teaching approach which brings vision, hearing, articulation and movement into play does appear to result in improved assimilation and retention. It is obviously easier to apply this approach with younger children; but in a one-to-one remedial teaching situation it is still a viable proposition with older students.

The finger-tracing method has been found useful for helping a child overcome a reversal tendency in reading and writing as well as building up a basic sight vocabulary. However, multisensory approaches should not be regarded as panaceas for all reading and spelling ills. Not only are they very time consuming and therefore mainly applicable with the most severe cases of reading disability, but Gillespie and Johnson (1974) warn that with some handicapped children bombarding them with all modes of presentation may actually confuse them.

*Games and apparatus*

In almost all texts dealing with remedial or corrective reading teachers will find abundant encouragement to use games and word-building equipment as adjuncts to their programmes. Games, it is argued, provide an opportunity for the learners to practise and overlearn essential material which might otherwise become boring and dull. Such repetition is essential for children who learn at a slow rate or who are poorly motivated. The use of games and equipment may also be seen as 'non-threatening', serving a therapeutic purpose within a group or individual teaching situation.

There can be little doubt that well-structured games and apparatus can perform a very important teaching function. Word Bingo, Picture-to-Word Matching Set, Syllable Jigsaws, Word Wheels, Phonic Rummy Games, etc., can all help to develop word recognition, phonic knowledge and decoding skills. However it is essential that a specific game or piece of equipment has a clearly defined purpose and that it is matched with a genuine learning need in children who are to use it. The material should contribute to the objectives for the lesson, not detract from them. Too often games are used in a very random way, almost to amuse the children or to keep them occupied. While this may be justified on therapeutic grounds it cannot be defended pedagogically. A study carried out by Baker, Herman and Yeh (1981) with second and third grade children found that the unstructured use of games, puzzles and supplementary material was *negatively* related to achievement in reading and mathematics.

It is also important that the use of games or apparatus be closely monitored by an adult if time is not to be wasted by the children and if the material is to be used correctly.

## Listening to Children Read

Regardless of which approach or blend of approaches a teacher decides to use in working with individual children, listening to the child read aloud should be an essential part of the programme. It permits the teacher to monitor such features as self-correcting behaviour, use of context, word-attack skill, fluency and phrasing. This writer has found it valuable to use such time as a 'reading together' experience, rather than merely listening to the child read. Having selected an appropriate book the session may take the following form.

☐ You (the teacher) volunteer to read the first page or two while the child follows in his or her copy of the book. The teacher's fluent reading of the text serves not only to model appropriate expression and rate but allows the child to get the flavour of the story. Names of characters will have cropped up and topic-specific terms will have been encountered by the time the child's turn comes to read. Allow the child to finger-point to keep the place in the text if necessary, rather than become lost and left behind in the story.

☐ Now invite the child to read the next page or half-page. As you listen to the performance anticipate any difficult words and simply provide them to maintain, at this stage, continuity and meaning.

☐ Praise the child for the reading, then continue yourself with the next page.

☐ Again invite the child to read the next page, providing help only when necessary. Don't destroy continuity by suggesting that the child sound-out the word. You might, however, suggest that the child read the rest of the sentence if he can't get one word. This will usually enable the reader to self-correct or make a contextual guess.

☐ After reading at least four or five pages together in this way the child will feel that a significant part of the story has been read. Indeed the story content (plot) will be emerging and a few minutes may be spent in talking about the key points so far to aid recall and comprehension. (This approach might be contrasted with the typical classroom ritual of hearing a child read one page, then marking his card and putting the book away until the next day or later in the week. So little of the actual story is covered each day that it is almost impossible for the child to understand what it is really about. The least able readers suffer most in this system.)

☐ In later sessions the amount that you read is gradually reduced (but never totally withdrawn) allowing the child more time to perform independently. It is at this stage that you can gain insights into the child's skills by attending to the nature of miscues which may occur from time to time.

☐ It is important that a child be helped to read a *significant amount* at each session. By breaking into the vicious circle of 'I can't read well — so I avoid reading — so I don't get much practice — so I don't improve', you are able to prove to the child that he or she is, indeed, making progress. Some form of daily charting of pages read can be very useful here.

It is important to aim to make the child an *independent* reader. The amount of correction and feedback given to a low ability reader may tend to maintain that child's dependence on adult support and guidance. Frequently the feedback tends to be drawing the child's attention to the phonic properties of a word, or simply supplying the word, rather than helping the reader to pick up cues from context and thus become more independent in performance. Less frequent and less direct support seems to provide more opportunity for the child to self-correct and maintain attention to meaning (McNaughton: 1981).

## Improving Comprehension

As long ago as 1969 Nila Banton Smith identified four levels of comprehension, each level containing a cluster of component skills and each being dependent upon competence at the previous levels. The most basic level is referred to as *Literal Comprehension* (understanding, at least superficially, the basic information which is being presented). This level is dependent upon such subskills as: recognition of main idea, grasp of sequence and order of detail, recognition of cause and effect relationships when these are stated in the text. To a large extent even this level depends upon the learner's own previous knowledge and experience. If the concepts being presented are very new even literal comprehension and recall will be difficult. This raises the question 'Is reading a text the best way of introducing a new and unfamiliar topic?' For some learners the answer is certainly 'No'.

The second level of comprehension is *Interpretation* and is concerned with going beyond what is actually presented in the text, inferring and reading between the lines and drawing conclusions. Subskills at this level include: making generalisations, predicting outcomes, reasoning cause-effect when these are not stated, discovering relationships.

The third level of comprehension is *Critical Reading*. This involves judgement of the quality, value, accuracy and truthfulness of what is read, detecting bias or over-statement. The final level is referred to as *Creative Reading*. At this level the reader goes beyond the writer's material and generates new ideas or develops new insights which were not explicit in the text.

It is argued that in many classrooms comprehension exercises rarely demand responses other than at the literal (factual recall) level. While this level *is* important since it is basic to the other three levels, a programme which sets out to develop comprehension skills in children should include questions (oral or written) which demand some thinking at the interpretive, critical and creative levels. For example, following a short story about the crash of a passenger aircraft these questions might be posed.

- ☐ How many passengers escaped the crash? (Literal)
- ☐ Why did the failure of the cabin pressure lead to the crash? (Interpretive)
- ☐ From the way he behaved before the crash what kind of man to you think the pilot was and could his judgement be trusted? (Critical)
- ☐ Many air crashes involving loss of life occur each year. How might flight be made a safer method of transport? (Creative)

If a child has difficulties in comprehending what is read, particularly at the first two levels, it is worth considering whether there is a serious mismatch between his or her own vocabulary knowledge and the words being used to convey the information in the text. A child may be able to read a word correctly but not know (or may misunderstand) its meaning. In such cases there is a need to devote more time to word study and vocabulary building when comprehension activities are used in classroom.

Children who read very slowly or much too fast often comprehend poorly. Attention to rate of reading is thus indicated as a remedial intervention.

For some children the actual recall of information is poor. Recall is dependent upon attention, vividness of content, intention to remember, rehearsal, and any connections with the reader's previous experience. These factors may help to identify why a particular child is having problems.

The following suggestions may help to improve comprehension.

- ☐ Ensure that the material presented is interesting to the child and at an appropriate readability level.

84

☐ For the more limited learners make frequent use of 'Instruction Sheets' which the child must read, interpret and act upon; for example, carrying out simple experiments, following a recipe, making a model.

☐ Read through the comprehension questions *before* the story or passage is read so that the child enters the material knowing what to look for.

☐ Encourage children to set comprehension questions for each other; and then use these questions to discuss what is meant by critical reading, inferring, predicting, etc.

☐ Use daily newspapers and magazine articles as the basis for some classroom discussion and comprehension exercises. 'Highlighter' pens can be used to focus upon key ideas, important terms, facts to remember, etc. This is important for the development of study skills in secondary and tertiary education courses.

Much of value can be achieved in developing comprehension skills informally (Gillet & Bernard: 1985). The questioning and discussion based on a page or story just read with an individual or a group is a much more natural way of making the learner think about the actual ideas and information presented than is the case with formal comprehension exercises; although there is a place even for these if used to focus upon important comprehension strategies. Avoid using comprehension exercises as a twice-weekly ritual simply because they may appear on the time table.

For teachers wishing to discover more about the development of comprehension skills they should refer to Bader (1980) who devotes fifty pages of her book to this topic. For advice to parents on helping their children read with understanding at home see the book by Gillet & Bernard (1985). For a highly structured, step-by-step procedure for teaching comprehension skills see Gersten & Carnine (1986).

---

*SELF-TESTING EXERCISE 5.1*

*Review the teaching methods presented in this chapter. List those you would find useful in your present teaching situation.*

*Which of the techniques could be used with adults who have problems with literacy?*

---

## Remedial Programming: Some General Principles

Having selected appropriate methods and materials based on a thorough knowledge of the child with special needs, it is important to consider the general principles which need to be applied when designing an actual programme and when working with the child. The principles are well illustrated in the field of programmed instruction (e.g. computer-assisted learning). The principles are these:

☐ Create situations where the child must be *actively involved* since these are more likely to hold the child's attention and keep him or her on-task and productive.

☐ Simplify the learning task as much as possible by breaking down the material to be taught into *very carefully graded steps.*

☐ Each step in a learning task should be simple enough for the children to *succeed when they make an honest effort.*

☐ Provide *abundant reinforcement and reward* for genuine effort and progress. When possible, allow the children to plot their own progress on a chart to provide some form of *visual evidence of improvement.*

☐ Provide *corrective feedback* when errors occur or incorrect strategies are used. Then allow the children to *practise* the response until it is mastered.

☐ With slower learning children more *repetition* of the units of instruction is required before the material can be thoroughly assimilated and mastered. Teaching for these children will need a *greater degree of over-learning* (that is, continuing to teach and revise beyond the point at which the child first seems to grasp the idea). Repetition and over-learning are necessary, but must not be achieved at the expense of enjoyment. Carefully selected games and computer programmes provide opportunity for *repetition with interest and enjoyment.*

☐ There will be a need, in many cases, to *regain lost interest, confidence and motivation.* There may be merit in selecting an approach which is totally different from anything the child has encountered so far; and even gimmicks have their place here.

☐ Perhaps the most important ingredient to ensure enjoyment in learning is the *teacher's own personality and enthusiasm.* An enthusiastic teacher can make even a flashcard game exciting and enjoyable.

## Summary

In general, most remedial reading approaches do not differ greatly from mainstream approaches. Much useful help can be provided for many children with special needs simply by a *more careful and structured use of the regular class programme*. Where this is possible it is to be preferred to the use of more exotic and unusual techniques often requiring one-to-one tuition in a withdrawal room situation. However, some children's learning difficulties are so acute, or their attitude toward reading is so negative, that their needs can only be met by a carefully designed programme which requires methods and materials that differ markedly from those in regular use. This chapter has presented a reasonably broad spectrum of approaches covering these extremes, from those suitable for whole-class or group use to those appropriate for individual tutoring.

The books listed in the *Further Reading* section provide other practical suggestions.

When programming for remedial reading the teacher must constantly keep in mind that the *long-term* goal is to help the learner become an independent reader, capable of reading for pleasure and for information; or in the case of the very handicapped individual, reading for social survival. The teaching of phonic skills, word-attack and so forth must never become an end in itself, but must be recognised as a step on the ladder to fully functional reading ability.

## Further Reading

Aukerman, R. C. (1984) *Approaches to beginning reading (2nd ed)*. New York, Wiley.

Bader, L. A. (1980) *Reading diagnosis and remediation in classroom and clinic*. New York, Macmillan.

Bryant, L. & Bradley, P. (1985) *Children's reading problems*. Oxford, Blackwell.

Carnine, D. & Silbert, J. (1979) *Direct instruction reading*. Columbus, Merrill.

Cassell, C. (1982) *Teaching poor readers in the secondary school*. London, Croom Helm.

Gillet, S. & Bernard, M. (1985) *Reading rescue*. Hawthorn, A.C.E.R.

Goodman, Y. & Burke, C. (1980) *Reading strategies: focus on comprehension*. New York, Holt, Rinehart & Winston.

Hicks, C. (1986) Remediating specific reading disabilities: a review of approaches. *Journal of Research in Reading* 9 (1): 39-55.

Holdaway, D. (1979) *The foundations of literacy.* Sydney, Ashton Scholastic.

Lawrence, D. (1985) Improving self-esteem and reading. *Educational Research* 27 (3): 194-200.

McDonald, T. H. (1984) *First aid in reading, writing and spelling.* Sydney, Hale & Iremonger.

Miles, T. R. (1975) *More help for dyslexic children.* London, Methuen.

---

**Application**

*Using data obtained from a suitable assessment of an individual with reading problems (see Chapter 4) plan an appropriate remedial programme.*

*Try to implement the first six stages as set out in Figure 4.1 (page 48). Methods and materials may be selected from ideas in this chapter, or from your wider reading.*

*State your objectives in very precise terms in order that they may be used later to evaluate the success of your programme.*

---

# 6 FOSTERING DEVELOPMENT IN WRITING AND SPELLING

*'Learning to write involves coming to appreciate writing as a vehicle for discovering what to say. It involves learning to play around with language.'*
(Newman: 1984, p.495)

## Intoduction

Perhaps more than any other area of the curriculum creative writing presents problems for the slower learning child, the unmotivated child and the child with a learning disability. Certainly it is the most demanding of the language skills (Pinsent: 1984).

Contemporary approaches to the teaching of writing (e.g. Graves: 1983) have done much to alleviate the anxiety and frustration which, in years gone by, many of the slower or educationally handicapped students experienced whenever *'writing'* or *'composition'* appeared on the time table. To them it meant a silent period of sustained writing with little or no opportunity to discuss work or ask for assistance. Great importance was placed on accuracy and neatness at the first attempt and many children must have felt extremely inhibited. Even when the teacher wasn't a severe judge of the product, the children themselves often carried out self-diagnosis and decided that they couldn't write because their product was not perfect. This view was often reinforced by their parents. An attitude quickly developed in the child, 'I can't write'.

What is the change which has come about in recent years which now enables more children to *'experiment fearlessly'* through the medium of writing? The change has been one of a shift in emphasis from *'the finished product'* to the actual *process of composing and revising*. The method is represented best in the *'process-conference approach'* of Donald Graves which will be described in a moment. It seems that the impact which this educator and his colleagues have had upon classroom practice in such a very short space of time is quite dramatic when compared with the usual changes or innovations in education which commonly take up to ten years before they influence teaching behaviour. Graves et al were researching in 1978-80 and publishing in 1981. By 1982 a very high percentage of primary teachers appeared not only to know of the *'process-conference approach'* but were actually implementing it in their classrooms. It is likely that part of its ready acceptance was due to the way in which it neatly complemented contemporary psycholinguistic views on the teaching of reading (i.e. children learn to read mainly by reading for meaning; and children learn to write by writing for some real purpose). The ability of Graves to spell out the *practical* implications of this research in terms which teachers could readily apply was also a very important feature: teachers could immediately use his ideas.

## The Process-Conference Approach

Briefly, the process-conference approach embodies the following principles.

☐ Writing, as a process, usually involves a number of separate stages, from the initial hazy formulation of ideas to the first written draft, through subsequent revision and editing to a final product (although not *all* writing should be forced to pass through all stages).

☐ The choice of topic should usually be made by the writer. Personal narrative is likely to result in the most lively and relevant communications.

☐ A child writing in a classroom has a potential audience in not only the teacher but also the peer group. A friend or partner can be used as a sounding board for ideas and can read, discuss and make suggestions for written drafts. *'. . . teachers who enable children to help each other, provide not only important service in immediate child help, but a unique chance to learn more about writing by helping another person. Children in this situation are able to use language to talk about writing more specifically'* (Graves: 1981, p.203).

☐ The teacher should confer with each and every child about the writing being produced. This involves far more than the automatic dispensation of praise and encouragement: and it will involve quite different amounts of time and advice according to individual needs and abilities. Graves deals with this very important issue in his chapter *'Questions Teachers Ask About Conferences'.*

☐ Teachers themselves should write in the classroom and thus demonstrate the composing, editing and publishing stages in action.

☐ When possible and appropriate children's work should be 'published' for a wider audience (class book, display board, school library, etc.).

How should teachers interpret and apply these principles for children who have extreme difficulty in achieving success in written language?

90

Children who exhibit difficulties in written expression fall into one of two groups. The groups are not mutually exclusive and there is overlap. Each group calls for rather different instructional strategies. The first group comprises those children of any age level who have general difficulties in learning to read, write and spell because either they are slower learners (perhaps even mildly intellectually disabled) or they are of normal intelligence but have a genuine disability when dealing with language in written or printed form. In both cases a lack of ability accounts for their current problems and the teacher needs to make any writing task clear and simple enough to ensure success when the child is given additional help and guidance. The second group comprises those children of any age who can write *but don't,* the reluctant and unmotivated students. These children appear not to see the relevance of writing or have not experienced the excitement of written communication and get no satisfaction from it. Some of these students may have encountered negative or unrewarding experiences during the early stages of becoming writers and thus acquired what has been termed 'writing apprehension' which now causes them to avoid the task whenever possible (Auten: 1983). Their problem is one of poor motivation leading to habitually low levels of productivity. Here the teacher must regain lost interest and build confidence. Some practical suggestions to assist with the teaching of both categories will now be offered.

## Providing Special Assistance

### Slower learners and those with learning problems

The classroom atmosphere which encourages all children to experiment and take risks in their writing without fear of criticism or ridicule is a very necessary (but in itself insufficient) condition for the least able students. In many cases, particularly with the upper primary or secondary student with a history of bad experiences in writing, simply creating the atmosphere is not enough; more than the ordinary amount of guidance and encouragement from the teacher will also be needed. Indeed, Graves (1983) describes some such children in his chapters titled *'How to help children catch up'* and *'How to help children with special problems of potential.'* His studies of ways in which very young children begin to write and compose help to throw some light on the performance and needs of older children with difficulties in writing (Graves: 1981). In particular these studies indicate how important it is to view a child's writing attempts *diagnostically,* to determine how much a child can achieve

91

unaided, to observe what strategies he/she brings to composing, spelling and revising.

---

*SELF-TESTING EXERCISE 6.1*

*If you have access to a class of young children who have not been in school very long try to collect some samples of their attempts at 'free writing'.*
*What does the material tell you about their grasp of written language?*
*Is most of the spelling intelligible? What does the spelling tell you about their emerging knowledge of word structure?*
*Do you consider that 'invented' spelling should be encouraged in young beginning writers and with slower learners of any age?*

---

With some slow learning children the initial stimulus for writing may have to come from the teacher rather than from free choice. The notion of a teacher setting the topic is *not* against the philosophy of Graves. On the other hand, some children will have interests and experiences about which they can talk freely and can then be helped to write. The link here with the language-experience approach to reading for such children should be obvious: *'What I know about I can talk about. What I can talk about someone can help me to write. What I have written I can read'.*

Graves (1983) suggests the following possible sequence in assisting a child with difficulties to produce something satisfying. In addition he says that such children need to be *helped daily* and usually during the *first ten minutes* of the lesson.

☐ Initial 'warm up' — perhaps a few minutes spent with handwriting patterns or letter formation.
☐ Copying of something previously written.
☐ Discussion of new topic for writing.
☐ Drawing the topic.
☐ Further discussion with teacher.
☐ Composing one or two sentences.
☐ Feedback from the teacher.

With children of limited ability or those lacking in confidence, the teacher may have to structure very tightly the discussion at various stages even to the extent of writing down key vocabulary and possible sentence beginnings for the child to use. Graves advises teachers not to be afraid of saying, at times, *'Try doing it this way . . .'* Teachers are still permitted to teach! However, during the discussion and feedback stages (the 'conferring') the teacher should not over-correct, but rather encourage the child to talk and to think. The main aim is to help the child generate ideas and then to sort these into an optimum sequence.

In the early stages it is important not to place undue stress upon accuracy of spelling since this can stifle the child's attempts at communicating ideas freely. Invented spelling gives children the freedom to write with attention to content and sequence. Charles Cripps (1983) makes an excellent point when he says, *'. . . it is essential that a misspelling is never referred to as something "wrong" but instead as something nearly right'* *(p.22).* As the child becomes more confident and productive the teacher, while still remaining supportive, will make the conferring stage rather less structured. Enabling-type questions are still used to extend the child's thinking and to build upon the writing so far produced. Searle (1984) uses the term 'scaffolding' to suggest this surreptitious support which can be reduced gradually. In the case of the least able children, particularly in upper primary and secondary classes, it will be mainly the teacher who monitors the child's work-in-progress and who has most to offer when they confer. Extreme care must be exercised in using peers to read and comment upon the writing of other children with difficulties. In some classrooms able children will have a sufficiently positive attitude towards children who are less able and can offer very useful assistance in a peer-tutoring role. In other classrooms, or in some individual cases, the able writer may be inclined to ridicule any naive contributions and thus rapidly undermine the confidence and motivation of the slower child. Peer critiquing is often written about and talked about as if it is a simple strategy to employ in the classroom but actually it needs to be done with great sensitivity. Teachers must spend time in modelling the critiquing process before expecting children to implement it skilfully: e.g. how to highlight the good points, how to detect what is not clear, how to help with the generation of new ideas, how to assist with adding or deleting material and polishing the work.

Since the foundation of the approach depends so much upon the child-writer having someone with whom to confer it is important to consider other possible sources of assistance. Mention has already been made of the teacher and the peer group. Teacher aides, older students, college students and parent-helpers can all be of assistance. In all cases these helpers must know what their role is and will require some informal training by the teacher if they are not to adopt an approach which is too didactic.

It is important particularly at high school level to have all subject specialists participate in assisting children to develop writing skills (Sewell: 1982). Composing and revising should not be confined to lessons marked as 'English' on the time table.

### Some specific strategies

In helping children generate ideas and compose in writing Humes (1983) suggests that they be taught a framework of questions which can be used if necessary during the initial stages of planning. E.g. *'What happened first?' 'Where did it happen?' 'To whom did it happen?' 'What happened next?'* etc. Self-directed questions such as *'What does it look like?* (size, colour, shape, etc.)', *'What does it feel like?',* will help children become more descriptive in their writing. These temporary props are very useful for slower children but they must not be allowed to become utterly dependent upon such starting points.

Another strategy suggested by Humes (1983) is that of *'Shuffling Ideas'.* As ideas for writing are generated each is written quickly on a separate card and finally the cards are reordered until the most suitable and appealing sequence is obtained. The sequence can become the focal point for discussion between teacher and child or between two children. The procedure avoids the problem which sometimes occurs when a child is asked to revise a draft written in full on a single page, and it does help to establish the idea of planning and revising. *'When students overcome the idea that the first draft is the only draft, they become revisers'* (Humes: 1983, p.13).

To assist with the development of revising and editing skills Humes suggests that the whole class (or a small group of students) might look at a duplicated essay or one displayed on an overhead projector and make suitable alterations and improvements to it after discussion.

Another useful related activity is that of *'sentence combining'.* Often the slower students will tend to write very short sentences, lacking fluency and variety.

E.g.   *I saw Norwood play on Saturday.*
        *They beat the Panthers by 16 points.*
        *Button got injured.*
        *It was in the first quarter.*

These sentences can be combined in various ways.

E.g.    *'On Saturday I saw Norwood beat the Panthers by 16
points. The only bad part was in the first quarter when
Button was injured.'*

Suitable exercises can be devised to help children develop skills
in combining sentences.

Many of the less able children have, in the past, written very
little during times set aside for writing. This is part of the vicious
circle which might be described thus: *'I don't like writing so
I don't write much, so I don't get much practice, so I don't write
much . . . etc.'* Humes (1983) has advocated frequent writing
practice (daily) and even to the extent of using 'speed writing'
against a time limit (e.g. for 5 mins.), with children copying
existing material as rapidly as possible to convince them that
they can indeed 'write a lot' when style and accuracy are not
to be judged. A modified form of precision teaching can even
be used to increase output of some students. The number of
words written or sentences completed in the allotted time during
writing lessons can be counted and charted each day. Again,
even this rather formal imposition is not condemned by Graves
(see Graves: 1983 p.208).

Small booklets are usually better than exercise books for
slower children. The opportunity to make a fresh start almost
every week is far better than being faced with the accumulation
of evidence of past failures which can accrue in an exercise
book. For students of all ages a loose-leaf folder may be very
useful as a replacement for the traditional exercise book. There
is a place for the daily diary, journal or news book; but teachers
should avoid such writing becoming merely habitual, repetitive
and at times poorly constructed 'garbage' (Auten: 1983). There
is a danger of this being the case even with children who can
write well.

Leading from the points above it is obvious that our notion
of 'free writing' for the least able students should be interpreted
as 'freely guided writing' in the early stages. Quite original ideas
may be there but the process of organising them before getting
them down on paper needs to be teacher-supported. As
confidence and proficiency increase with the passage of time
the amount of direct help can be greatly reduced for most
students.

95

## Reluctant writers

For the teacher the priority here is to modify the negative attitude the student has developed towards writing. This basically means capturing the child's interest in some form of written communication which will bring rewards and satisfaction for that particular child.

---

### ANECDOTE

I recall that one student I taught in an upper primary class was loath to expend any energy at all in writing. He had acquired a very functional repertoire of avoidance strategies and could usually outwit my attempts to get him to put pen to paper. More by chance than design this boy happened to make an incredibly successful puppet in a craft lesson and he was genuinely proud of the result. I suggested that it would be useful if he could prepare a poster with illustrations and instructions so that others could benefit from his skills and could make similar puppets. This ruse worked and the boy produced a most thoughtful and well-sequenced piece of writing. (It would be pleasant to be able to report that from that moment he became a keen writer; but in reality we continued to have long periods of poor productivity with very occasional bursts of enthusiasm. It illustrates that it is not always easy to find topics which will motivate reluctant writers but we have a duty to keep up the search.) (Westwood: 1985.)

---

## Video or film scripts

Much use is made of improvised drama in both primary and secondary classrooms, drama requiring no scripts. A useful variation is to get the students, particularly the reluctant writers, to prepare a script in detail and then film or record the action after rehearsal. The combination of practical work, writing and production of something which can then be seen and discussed is usually adequate stimulus for even the most reluctant student.

## Book production

Extending the earlier suggestion of small booklets it is useful to have the students prepare somewhat more ambitious products. The following topics are particularly motivating for reluctant writers.

'*A book about myself*' — My family, Where I live. What I do. Things I like. Things I hate. My friends. The book can also include factual material: e.g. height, weight, pulse rate, etc.

'*A book about this school*' — Descriptions. Photos. Plans. Interviews with teachers.

'*A book about my class*' — Descriptions. Photos. Interviews.

'*Our book of jokes*' — Don't forget to censor these before parent evening!

'*Our neighbourhood*' — Location. Personalities. Shops. Industries. Entertainment.

'*Our visit to . . .*' — Impressions and summaries following fieldtrips and excursions. (Don't make this a regular feature of every trip or you will find yourself in the position of the old joke where a class was on an excursion and two children saw a flying saucer land in a field. 'Sir! Sir!', one child began. 'Shut up you fool!' said the other 'We'll only have to write about it'.)

### Letter writing and project exchange between schools

It is very useful indeed to set up an exchange system between schools, particularly if one school is in the city and one in the country. It can start out as a 'pen pal' scheme but extend to exchange of class books, project materials, etc., and even result in visits between schools.

### 'You write the rest' stories

---

### ANECDOTE

One technique which I used when teaching in special classes was to prepare a story about a popular character currently appearing on children's television. The story is told or read to the class for enjoyment; but just when you get to a cliff-hanger climax the story stops. What happens next? Individuals can write their own episode or you can brainstorm ideas from the group.

I found it particularly useful to type a simplified version of the story I had read to the children, spreading this over several half-pages of a small booklet and providing a frame for an illustration above each passage of print. The children, who were not proficient readers, could cope with the simplified material since it dealt with a story just read to them; the plot was familiar. The second half of the

Continued next page

---

*Anecdote (cont.)*

booklet was blank to allow the children to write their own endings and provide illustrations. This example was from a Doctor Who story. Teacher's story ends with this paragraph: *'He was in for a shock when he switched on the televiewer. The giant spiders were spinning a web over the Tardis. The strands looked as strong as rope. Suddenly the lights went out. He dashed to the controls and frantically flicked the switches. Nothing happened. The Tardis refused to move. They were trapped!!!'* . . .

Patricia's story continues: *'Dr. Who was cross. The spiders sat on the Tardis and sang a jungle song. Dr. Who took the plants he had collected and did an experiment on them. The plants turned into little people. The Doctor put the little people outside and they began to chew through the web. Soon the wind came and the web blew away. The Tardis was free again.'* (Westwood: 1985)

## Comic strips

Comics and cartoons can be useful for getting retarded or emotionally disturbed children to write short assignments. They are pleased with the quick, tangible results.

The most popular comic strips from the newspaper can be utilised since these tend to have no more than four or five frames of information. Using correcting fluid the teacher can white-out the original words in the 'speech balloons'. After brief discussion with an adult or peer the child can suggest suitable comments which each character might be making and can be helped to write these in the spaces. A number of such cartoon strips can be pasted into a class book for general use.

## Word processors

The arrival of word processors in classrooms has provided yet another avenue for children to gain confidence in composing, editing, erasing and publishing their own material (Newman: 1984). The use of the word processor is particularly applicable for reluctant writers.

*SELF-TESTING EXERCISE 6.2*

*Plan a programme which might be of assistance in helping a ten-year-old child improve his or her attitude towards story writing and, at the same time, increase the child's work output and attainment in the area of writing.*

refers to lists of words which individual children actually use and need in their writing, the answer is certainly 'yes'. If the lists are based on other criteria, e.g. words grouped according to visual or phonemic similarity, the decision to use such a list with a particular student or group of students must be made in the light of their specific learning needs as indicated above.

The value of lists or word groups is that they may help the student to establish an awareness of common letter sequences, e.g. *-ight; -ought*. This awareness may help a student take a more rational approach to tackling an unfamiliar word. The limitation of formal lists is that they always fail to supply a particular word a student needs at the appropriate time. The most useful list from the point of view of the weakest spellers will be one compiled according to personal needs and common errors. The list might be given the unofficial title *'Words I find difficult.'* A copy of this list can be kept in the back of the student's exercise book and used when he or she is writing a rough draft or proof-reading a final draft of a piece of written work.

## Some final points

When planning a remedial programme in spelling the following points should be kept in mind.

- [ ] For the least able spellers *daily* attention will be needed, with weekly revision and testing for mastery.
- [ ] Over a period of time collect a list of words frequently needed by children to whom you are giving special help. Use this list for regular review and assessment.
- [ ] Once a special programme is established students should always work on specific words misspelled in free writing lessons as well as on more general word lists or word families.
- [ ] Since repetition and overlearning are important it is useful to have a range of games and word puzzles available to reinforce the spelling of important words. The games must be closely matched to the objectives of the programme or they may simply keep children amused without leading to mastery.
- [ ] The remedial teacher in the high school should try to give students help in spelling words from specific subject areas: e.g. *ingredients, temperature, chisel, theory, etc.*
- [ ] Use some form of visual record of improvement, an individual progress chart or simple graph to indicate the number of new words mastered each week. Employ any gimmick which reinforces a student's awareness of the real progress being made.

103

☐ When making a correction to a word a student should rewrite the whole word not merely erase the incorrect letters.

☐ The value of having students spell words aloud is very questionable where the alphabet names rather than the sounds are used. Spelling is essentially a writing activity. The visual appearance and the flow of the sequence of written letters provide important clues to the speller which are absent when a word is spelled aloud.

☐ Margaret Peters is adamant that a neat, careful style of handwriting which can be executed swiftly and easily by the student is an important factor associated with spelling ability. It cannot be inferred that good handwriting *per se* causes good spelling; but laboured handwriting and uncertain letter formation almost certainly inhibit the easy development of spelling habits at an automatic response level (Peters: 1967).

---

*SELF-TESTING EXERCISE 6.3*

*Write a brief article for a parents' magazine indicating ways in which spelling can be taught in a mixed-ability class of children in the age range 7 years to 9 years. Also suggest strategies parents might use to assist their children to improve in spelling skills.*

---

**CASE STUDY**

**A child with spelling difficulties: 'Bevan'. Age 9 yrs 11 mths.**

**Evaluation of performance**

*Bevan's result on the spelling test suggests that his spelling ability is currently at the level of an average student in the age range 7 years 9 months to 8 years 0 months. As he is of average verbal ability in other respects this represents a degree of spelling retardation of roughly two years.*

*It is important to note in this context that his reading age is only 8 years 10 months, suggesting that his difficulties are not solely with spelling. The informal phonic survey indicates that Bevan has a reasonable grasp of basic and intermediate phonic skills. There was some specific difficulty with the blends 'tw', as in twelve and twist (he sounded the 'tw' as 'th'), and with 'dr' as in draw and dragon. He is not at complete mastery level with higher-order phonic skills such as syllabification; and he lacks the ability to recognise more difficult letter clusters such as '. . . ough', '. . . ious' and '. . . dge'.*

He falls into the category of students described as having poor powers of visual perception and is over-compensating by using a predominantly phonetic approach. Unfortunately his higher-order phonic skills are inadequate to enable him to cope with the more complex words in reading or spelling. Bevan is not very skilled in analysing the component sounds in complex words, frequently failing to identify certain phonemes when attempting to break words down and therefore omitting them in his spelling. At the moment he has not been trained to go back and check the visual appearance of the word to see if it 'looks' correct.

The diagnostic tests indicate clearly that Bevan lacks a functional spelling vocabulary of **irregular** words. He managed to spell only one word correctly in a particular list dictated today. He produces such errors as 'orful' (awful), 'engin' (engine), 'shor' (sure), 'captin' (captain) and 'frend' (friend). There is only one way to learn to spell common irregular words and that is through abundant repetition and overlearning until they are mastered to the point of being automatic habit responses.

In addition to the advice above one strategy Bevan **must** develop is to proof-read his own written work before passing it in for marking. He was able to identify and correct without assistance more than 50% of the errors in a dictation passage today. He was also able to correct many of the mistakes in the written work in his school exercise book. If he does this for himself every time it is much more useful than having an essay or story returned with a large number of corrections provided by the teacher (particularly since Bevan doesn't appear to do anything with the corrected words in terms of learning or remediation).

He may find it very useful to build up a list of words which he frequently gets wrong or finds difficult. This can be written on a card and kept in the back of his exercise book and used as an aid to proof-reading.

Bevan should **write words several times** as an essential part of his word study. Do not allow letter-by-letter copying of a word, but get him to reproduce the complete flow and sequence of letters at a single attempt. When making corrections he should **rewrite the whole word**, not alter the letter or letters. He has a tendency to omit letters from certain

105

*words and it is of no help in learning those words merely to insert the missing letter (with an arrow) as he was doing today.*

*He needs to work hard at his handwriting. He can produce a very neat cursive style if he makes the effort, but this has not yet developed to the level of swift, automatic movement. His print script breaks down hopelessly under speed. Research has shown that the ability to write swiftly and neatly in a joined hand is a definite aid to spelling development.*

*Finally, I do not consider that Bevan has a spelling 'disability' in the clinical sense. He simply lacks appropriate strategies to help himself in a rational manner. He can be taught these strategies and his spelling ability should improve, at least to the level of his reading (word recognition) ability.*

## Summary

This chapter has provided practical suggestions for helping poorly motivated and slower learning students to write and to spell. Most of these techniques can be used within the normal classroom setting and require only minor modifications to the mainstream language arts programme.

The reader will have noted in this and earlier chapters the importance placed upon *the teacher modelling effective ways of approaching a task,* whether it be composing and editing a story or attempting to learn how to spell a new word. A very large part of remedial education for children with special needs should be designed to improve their task-approach skills since these are often poorly developed and therefore contribute to educational failure. Alongside this priority there is also need to help these children feel good about the work they produce and the improvements they make. Hopefully, this chapter has further illustrated ways of making this possible.

## Further Reading

Graves, D. (1983) *Writing: teachers and children at work.* Exeter, Heinemann.

Haley-James, S. (1981) *Perspectives on writing in Grades 1-8.* Urbana, National Council of Teachers of English.

Hodges, R. E. (1982) *Improving spelling and vocabulary in the secondary school.* Urbana, National Council of Teachers of English.

McIlroy, K. (1980) *Helping the poor speller (2nd ed)*. Auckland, Heinemann.

Peters, M. L. (1985) *Spelling: caught or taught? A new look (2nd ed)*. London, Routledge.

Petty, W. & Jensen, J. (1980) *Developing children's language*. Boston, Allyn & Bacon.

Smedley, D. (1983) *Teaching the basic skills: spelling, punctuation and grammar*. London, Methuen.

Torbe, M. (1978) *Teaching spelling*. London, Ward Lock.

Whitehead, M. (1985) On learning to write: recent research on developmental writing. *Curriculum* 6 (2): 12-19.

---

**Application**

*Study the results on the next page from a girl who attempted two diagnostic spelling tests A and B (below) and a standardised spelling test.*

*What do her errors suggest as possible priority needs for remediation?*

### DIAGNOSTIC TESTS

*SET A*

*Regular Words*

| | | |
|---|---|---|
| *wet* | *van* | *rod* |
| *win-ter* | *thun-der* | *re-mind* |
| *re-port-er* | *un-der-stand* | *mem-ber-ship* |
| *un-ex-pect-ed-ly* | *rep-re-sent-ation* | *cel-e-bra tion* |

*SET B*

*Irregular Words*

| | | | |
|---|---|---|---|
| *ask* | *our* | *use* | *they* |
| *word* | *climb* | *laugh* | *because* |
| *awful* | *juice* | *dodge* | *stitch* |
| *ache* | *cruel* | *stomach* | *separate* |

| | | |
|---|---|---|
| on | do | eny |
| hot | hoo | grate |
| cup | here | shor |
| van | ship | wimin |
| jam | chop | anser |
| lost | food | bootifull |
| sit | fire | orkestre |
| plan | thin | ekule |
| mub | dat | appreeseate |
| beg | seem | familer |
| the | dart | enthew |
| gow | lowd | |
| for | from | |
| sow | eiy | |
| me | fite | |
| ar | frend | |
| of | dun | |

---

A. wet    van    rod
winter    thunder    remind
reporter    understand    membership
unexpectdly    representashun    selebraysh

B. ask    koure    youse    thay    werld
orfull    clim    larf    joos    doge
stick    ak    krewll    stumok    cep

# 7 GUIDING DEVELOPMENT IN BASIC MATHEMATICS

*The reasons for under-achievement in mathematics are many and varied. Apart from specific handicaps such as cerebral palsy, hearing or sight impairment, the reasons may fall into two broad categories — deficiencies in cognitive functioning and deficiencies in affective functioning . . . (The slow learner) is likely to be deficient in both these areas.'*

(Berrill: 1982, p.109)


## Introduction

Many mainstreamed handicapped children experience difficulty in acquiring number concepts and coping with the demands of calculation and problem solving. For example, in the case of some *physically handicapped* children perceptual difficulties, poor manipulative skills and restricted concrete experiences are frequently given as reasons for their weakness in arithmetic. Children with restricted life experiences who develop and learn at a slow rate may fail to develop an informal awareness of the number system prior to school entry (something most non-handicapped children have achieved by the age of four years: Ginsburg & Baroody: 1983). To this one must add that many of these children, e.g. those with spina bifida and hydro-cephalus, may spend very frequent periods of time in hospital for treatment or surgery and thus lose the continuity of learning in what is the most hierarchical subject in the curriculum. Almost all *intellectually disabled* children experience great difficulty in coping with the most basic arithmetic due to the abstract symbolic nature of the recording required for even simple operations. When attempting to carry out problem solving they may select totally inappropriate operations to perform (Janke: 1980), being unable to determine whether to add or subtract, multiply or divide. The mildly retarded individuals may remain at a concrete level of reasoning into their adult life. The moderately retarded may never progress beyond a pre-operational cognitive level. Even slow learners (who are not usually regarded as intellectually disabled) may remain at a concrete operational level until the later years of secondary schooling (Richards: 1982). Evidence of this may be seen in their tendency to finger-count or to use tally marks when performing calculations. This writer observed a first year high school student who, when faced with the problem $73 - 29 = $ , drew 73 tally marks in the margin of his page,

109

then crossed off 29 and counted those remaining; an effective but inappropriate strategy in terms of time and effort.

Any children with *language problems* (e.g. hearing impaired children) will also experience difficulties in solving word problems where the specific mathematical terminology may be misunderstood. Language difficulties in mathematics may also reflect significant *cultural differences* in otherwise bright and able children (Sayers: 1983). These children may cope adequately with arithmetic while it remains at a visual and concrete level. *'Mathematics teachers, generally well-versed in the language of mathematics, often fail to understand the confusion and frustration experienced by pupils trying to use this language'* (Monroe: 1977, p.28).

Not infrequently the instruction given in mathematics is poor in that it does not match the current aptitude or learning rate of the slower children. For example, the following six factors are indicative of poor quality instruction.

☐ At some stage in the children's schooling the teacher's pacing of the work has outstripped their ability to assimilate the concepts and skills and they have been left hopelessly behind.

☐ There was so little structuring of a 'discovery learning' situation that they failed to abstract or remember anything from it. A report in Britain (Cockcroft: 1982) indicates that for many children the value in experiential learning will be lost unless the follow-up is carefully structured and consolidated.

☐ The teacher's use of language in explaining mathematical relationships or posing questions may not have matched the children's level of comprehension.

☐ Abstract symbols may have been introduced too early in the absence of concrete materials or real-life examples; or concrete aids may have been removed too soon for some children. Lovell (1971) has said that there is a danger in forcing abstraction on children in advance of their understanding and experience. The children will either assimilate this with distortion or turn away from it in distaste. It is only too easy to make children hate mathematics!

☐ The children's grasp of simple relationships in number may not have been fully developed before larger numbers involving complications of place-value were introduced.

☐ The children may also have reading difficulties and, therefore, have been condemned to a diet of 'pure arithmetic' because they couldn't read the problems in the text book. Teaching only a set of computational tricks does not amount to efficient remedial teaching (Cockcroft: 1982). Such tricks are usually rapidly forgotten since they do not constitute meaningful learning.

So, there exists a variety of reasons to account for some children experiencing difficulty in mastering the facts, concepts and operations in arithmetic and applying these successfully to problem solving. While this information helps us to appreciate why a child has difficulties it is not usually particularly helpful to spend a great deal of time in attempting to track down the specific causal factors in individual cases; rarely will these indicate what should be done to assist the child. As with reading, writing and spelling, the most practical approach regardless of the child's handicap is to ascertain what he or she can already do in this area of the curriculum, to locate any specific gaps which may exist and to determine what he or she needs to be taught next. In other words, the *diagnostic model* presented in Figure 4.1 (Chapter 4) can be applied to assessment of skills in arithmetic and to guide programme planning in mathematics.

**Diagnosis**

With modern approaches to the teaching of mathematics (e.g. individual progression; discovery or enquiry methods) the need for regular assessment of individual progress for all students is greater than ever before. Periodic checks on the child's understanding of new work are essential; and such checks must usually involve working directly with the child to detect strengths and weaknesses in performance. Without this the teacher has little idea whether the pupil carries out an activity in rote fashion, through the help of other children, or with partial or complete understanding (Lovell: 1971). Keeping a record of children's progress along different paths in mathematics is a much greater challenge to the teacher now than it was with the traditional system in which one needed only to record the place each child had reached in a sequence which all were following.

Stage 1 in the diagnostic evaluation of mathematical skills may involve formal testing of the child using published or teacher-made tests to determine in general the level at which the child is functioning. Examination of the child's exercise books will provide further information. Follow-up diagnostic tests may then be employed to find precisely how much arithmetical and mathematical knowledge the child has and can apply.

A *task-analytic* approach may be taken when attempting to find the point of failure or misunderstanding in basic arithmetical processes. Several of the diagnostic number tests which have been in schools for many years are still valid and actually adopt this approach. By carefully grading the various steps involved in, say, long division, and providing test items to sample the child's competence at each stage, the teacher can detect the precise point of breakdown in computational skills or understanding. An analysis of the actual errors made by the child can then further pinpoint the teaching which needs to be done (Engelhardt: 1982. Sowder et al: 1986).

There are various levels of abstraction involved in diagnostic work in mathematics (Underhill, Uprichard & Heddens: 1980). To a large extent identification of these levels will help the teacher to answer the question, 'What can the child do in mathematics if given a little help and guidance?' The levels are: (i) concrete (ii) semi-concrete (iii) abstract. At the concrete level the child may be able to solve a problem or complete a process correctly if permitted to manipulate real objects. At the semi-concrete level pictorial presentations of the objects, together with the symbols, are sufficient visual information to ensure success. At the abstract level the child must work with the symbols only, either in printed form or as orally dictated by the teacher. During the diagnostic work with the child the teacher may move up or down within this hierarchy from abstract to concrete in an attempt to discover the level at which the child can succeed. Copeland (1974) provides some very useful examples of concrete level assessments for young or slower learning children.

It may be helpful to keep the following thoughts in mind when attempting to discover the child's present functional level. Referring to any items which a child fails to solve in a test or during deskwork following a period of instruction, ask yourself these questions:

☐ *Why* did the child get this item wrong?

☐ Can he or she carry out the process if allowed to use concrete aids or count on fingers or use a number line, etc.?

☐ Can he or she explain to me what to do? Ask the child to work through the example aloud step by step. At what point does the child obviously misunderstand?

The value of this last procedure cannot be over-stressed. If a child *explains* to you how he or she tackles the problem you are likely to pick up at once the exact point of confusion and can teach from there (Richards: 1982). Too often we jump in and reteach the whole process but still fail to help the child recognise and overcome the precise difficulty.

Reisman (1972) strongly advocates that teachers construct their own informal mathematical skills inventory containing test items covering key concepts, knowledge and skills presented in earlier years together with essential material from the current year. Such an inventory can very conveniently indicate precisely what the child can and cannot do and will assist with the ordering of priorities for teaching. The following three levels of assessment may help the teacher to design appropriate assessment materials. It is likely that the first two levels will be the most applicable for children with learning difficulties.

## Three levels of assessment

### Level 1

If the child's performance in basic number is very poor consider the following points. At this stage almost all the assessments will need to be made at an individual level, using appropriate concrete materials, toys, pictures, number cards, etc.

- ☐ Check the child's grasp of *vocabulary* associated with number relationships (e.g. 'bigger than', 'altogether', 'less', 'share', etc.).
- ☐ Check the child's *conservation* of number.

Then check the following knowledge and skills in this order. Can the child

- ☐ sort objects given *one attribute* (colour, size, shape, etc.)?
- ☐ sort objects given *two attributes?*
- ☐ produce equal sets of objects by *one-to-one matching?*
- ☐ *count* correctly objects to ten? To twenty?
- ☐ *recognise numerals* to 10? To twenty?
- ☐ place number symbols in *correct sequence* to 10? to twenty?
- ☐ *write numerals* correctly from dictation to 10? To twenty?
- ☐ understand *ordinal values* (fifth, tenth, second, etc.)?
- ☐ perform *simple addition* with numbers below ten in written form (e.g. 3 + 5 = )? With or without apparatus?
- ☐ perform *subtraction* with numbers below 10 in written form?

113

    ☐ *count-on* in a simple addition problem?
    ☐ *answer simple oral problems* involving addition or subtraction with numbers below 10?
    ☐ *recognise coins and paper money* (1p 2p 5p 10p 50p £1 or 1c 2c 5c 10c 20c 50c $1.00 $2.00)?

---

### Level 2

If the child's performance in mathematics is slightly better than Level 1 consider the following areas:

Can the child
    ☐ carry out *simple mental addition* with numbers below 20?
    ☐ carry out *simple mental problem-solving* without use of finger-counting or tally marks?
    ☐ carry out *simple subtraction mentally* as above? Is there a marked difference between performance in addition and subtraction? (N.B. the *One-minute Basic Number Facts Tests* at the end of this chapter are useful here and can be administered to a whole class simultaneously if necessary.)
    ☐ perform both *vertical and horizontal forms* of simple addition? ( $3$ and $3 + 5 = $ ).
        $+5$
    ☐ understand the *commutative law* in addition (i.e. that the order of items to be totalled does not matter)? Does the child see for example that $5 + 3$ and $3 + 5$ are bound to give the same total? When counting on to obtain a total in such problems does the child always count the smaller number on to the larger; or are these problems always solved from the left to the right regardless? ($2 + 8 = 12 + 5 = $ ).
    ☐ understand *additive composition* (i.e. all the possible ways of producing a given set or total)? For example, 5 is $4 + 1, 3 + 2, 2 + 3, 1 + 4, 5 + 0$.
    ☐ understand the *complementary or reversible character of addition and subtraction?* ($7 + 3 = 10, 10 - 7 = 3, 10 - 3 = 7$).
    ☐ watch an operation demonstrated using concrete material and then *record this in written form?*
    ☐ *translate a written equation* into a practical demonstration (e.g. use unifix cubes to demonstrate $12 - 4 = 8$)?
    ☐ listen to a simple real-life situation described in words and then work the problem in written form? *(Seven people were waiting at the bus stop. When the bus came only three*

*could get on. How many were left to wait for the next bus?)* Use numbers below 20. Can the child work problems at this level mentally?

☐ *recognise* and *write* numerals to 50?

☐ *tell the time* to the nearest half-hour? Read a digital clock correctly?

☐ recite the *days of the week?* Recite the *months of the year?*

---

## Level 3

If the child is able to succeed with most of the items in the previous levels or if he/she seems reasonably competent in many areas of basic math consider these questions.

Can the child

☐ *read and write numbers to 100?* To 1000? Can he or she read and *write sums of money* correctly?

☐ *halve* or *double* numbers mentally?

☐ add money mentally? Give change by the counting-on method?

☐ recite the *multiplication tables* correctly and answer random facts from these tables?

☐ perform the correct procedures for *addition* of H T U and Th H T U. Without carrying? With carrying in any column?

☐ understand *place value* with T U? With H T U? With Th H T U? This is a very common area of difficulty and may need to be checked very carefully.

☐ perform the correct procedures for *subtraction* of H T U and Th H T U? Without exchanging in any column? With exchanging? It is important to note the actual method used by the child to carry out subtraction. Is it 'decomposition' using only the top line of figures; or the 'equal addition' method using top and bottom lines?

☐ perform the correct steps in the *multiplication* algorithm? To what level of difficulty?

☐ perform the correct steps in the *division* algorithm? To what level of difficulty?

☐ recognise *fractions:* ½ ¼ 3½ 7¼ ¹/₁₀ 5³/₁₀ 0.8 5.9 etc.

---

*SELF-TESTING EXERCISE 7.1*

*Prepare the materials and questions needed in order to carry out assessments at one of the three levels described above.*

*Devise a simple checklist to enable you to record an individual child's responses to your assessment items.*

*For Level 3 you may be able to locate published arithmetic tests to include in your assessment; but failing this, teacher-designed questions and items are perfectly acceptable. Don't forget to grade your items in each area carefully and where possible include several items at each level of difficulty.*

---

## Remediation

Clearly it is impossible within a single chapter to summarise remediation procedures across the complete field of mathematics. One must be selective and is helped in this by MacDonald's (1975) statement that in teaching mathematics to slower learners the two biggest hurdles to overcome will be *number fluency* and *problem solving*. These two areas will be developed in the following pages.

*Basic number concepts and skills*

*Conservation.* Basic to all number work is the concept of *conservation of number;* that is, a group or set composed of N separate items remains a set of that number regardless of how it is arranged or distributed. Up to the age of five or six years (and much later with disabled learners) the number of items in a set may appear to alter if the members are rearranged spatially. Experience has to be given to children to help them understand conservation of number and not to be misled by what their eyes seem to tell them. Much of the preschool and early school experience of sorting, counting, giving out materials, one-to-one matching of objects, etc., should be helping the basic concept of conservation to develop. For some children the process needs to be made more explicit.

The following activities and apparatus may help a child to develop the concept of conservation of number:

☐ teacher-made cards with pictures, dot patterns, shapes and so on, in different groupings can be sorted into sets of equal size (numbers in the sets should be below ten and no numerals will be introduced);

- matching or joining up various patterns with equal numbers of shapes presented on worksheets;
- counting activities to ten (or less) to establish one-to-one correspondence between the number rhyme 'one, two, three . . .' and the actual objects in given sets, and to establish 'equivalence' or 'difference' between sets;
- matching of objects (toys, unit blocks, etc.) with pictures or dot patterns containing different size groups.

The *vocabulary* of early number relationships needs to be introduced carefully and systematically alongside such experiences. For the least able students this vocabulary needs to be repeated and over-learned until completely mastered (for example: same, different, more than, less than, few, many, all, none, altogether, as many as). One must not allow a child's mathematical progress to be held back by lack of ability to verbalise; but the almost total inability to verbalise found in some children can be a major obstacle which must be overcome. If the child's understanding of the vocabulary associated with number and mathematics is very restricted greater attention must be given to teaching and over-learning the appropriate terms in a meaningful context. It is not just the vocabulary itself which is important but the syntactical patterns which accompany the verbalisations. For example, 'Are there more dogs than cats in the picture?' 'How many more cars than buses can you see?'

*Counting.* Counting is perhaps the most fundamental of all early number skills. As indicated in the previous section it can assist with the development of conservation of number. If this skill of counting is deficient it can only be taught and improved by direct instruction, working with the child alone or as a member of a small group. Perhaps the problem may be that the child fails to make a correct one-to-one correspondence between the word spoken in the 'number rhyme' and the objects touched in order. If the physical act of counting a set of objects appears to be difficult for the child manual guidance of his or her hands may be needed. For young or handicapped children the use of 'finger plays' and 'number rhymes and songs' may assist with the mastery of counting. Rote counting to ten and then to twenty should be given high priority in any special mathematics programme.

*Recognition of numerals.* The cardinal value of number symbols should, of course, be related to a variety of sets of different objects. Teachers can make numeral-to-group matching

117

games (the numeral 11 on a card to be matched with 11 birds, 11 kites, 11 cars, 11 dots, 11 tally marks, etc.). Also useful are teacher-made lotto cards containing a selection of the number symbols being taught or over-learned (1 to 10, or 1 to 20, or 25 to 50, etc.). When the teacher holds up a flashcard and says the number the child covers the numeral on the lotto card. At the end of the game the child must say each number aloud as it is uncovered on the card. Later these same lotto cards can be used for basic addition and subtraction facts, the numerals on the cards now representing correct answers to some simple question from the teacher (5 add 4 makes . . .? The number 1 less than 8 is . . .?).

Activities with number cards can also be devised to help children sort and arrange the numerals in correct sequence from 1 to 10, 1 to 20, etc. The early items in the *Unifix Mathematics Apparatus* can be useful at this stage (e.g. the *Inset Pattern Boards, Number Indicators, Number Line to 20)*.

The *writing of numerals* should be taught parallel to the above activities. Correct numeral formation should be established as thoroughly as correct letter formation in handwriting: this will reduce the incidence of reversals of figures in written recording.

*Recording.* There is a danger that a slow learning child will be expected to deal with symbolic number recording too early. Pictorial recording, tally marks, and dot patterns are very acceptable forms of representation for the young or very backward child. Gradually, the writing of number symbols will accompany such picture-type recording and then finally replace, it, by which time the cardinal values of the numerals are really understood.

*Number facts.* Ashcraft (1985) suggests that functional knowledge in arithmetic involves two major components (i) mastery of number facts which can easily be retrieved from memory (to 9 + 9 and 9 x 9) (ii) a body of knowledge about computational procedures. Both components are needed in typical arithmetic problem solving situations. Number facts are involved in all steps of the sub-routines carried out later in quite complex computations.

It is essential that children be helped to develop *habit recall* of the basic number bonds rather than having, for example, to calculate with fingers each time they need 7 + 3 = 10. Being able to recall number facts easily is important for two main

118

reasons, it makes calculation easier and it allows time for the deepening of understanding (Ginsburg & Baroody: 1983). Knowing number facts is partly a matter of rote learning (remembered through constant exposure) and partly a matter of grasping a rule (e.g. that zero added to any number doesn't change it: $3 + 0 = 3$, $13 + 0 = 13$, etc. or that if $7 + 3 = 10$ then $7 + 4$ must be 'one more than ten', etc.).

Many children with learning disabilities have problems in learning and recalling number facts and tables and require extra attention devoted to this key area (Jones et al: 1985). The following suggestions may help.

*Daily speed and accuracy sheets.* One must not underestimate the value of a daily worksheet to practise recall of number facts and tables for those children still needing such experience. Children should aim to increase their own scores each day in, say, a three-minute session, thus competing against themselves, not the class average. They are likely to get responses correct because they are working at their own rate (and can use counters, tally marks, etc., if necessary). This procedure is preferable to the daily session on the same 'ten mental problems' which can become nothing more than a morning ritual which only teaches some children how poor they are at rapid mental arithmetic.

Daily speed and accuracy practice can be applied to arithmetical computation skills beyond the simple number facts referred to so far. The worksheets can contain random samples of all four basic processes. When used in this way the teacher can often detect particular areas of weakness (for example, a particular table not known thoroughly) and can then design additional practice material for this gap in the child's knowledge.

Speed and accuracy sheets must not be allowed to become an end in themselves. It is vital that a child has the opportunity to apply number facts and arithmetic skills to problem solving.

*Number games.* Almost any simple game involving a scoring system can be used to practise recall of number facts or simple addition or subtraction. For example, (i) a skittle game can be played using empty bleach or cordial containers with a value (score) painted on each. The child has to add the value for any knocked down with each roll of the ball. (ii) A ringboard game can be made using cuphooks screwed into a baseboard which is then hung from the wall. Each hook has its own value marked on the board. Rubber rings from preserving jars are thrown

119

at the board and a player has to rapidly total his/her score. (iii) Battery-operated games (e.g. *The Little Professor*) are readily available and are pre-programmed to present number bonds in random order on a visual display. The child must key-in correct responses to move on through the game. Many computer programmes are now available for a similar purpose and most contain a corrective feedback element to the child who makes an incorrect response. They are often 'user friendly' and will respond to the child by name, which can be an added bonus for slower or poorly motivated children.

*Computation and algorithms.* Once children have evolved their own meaningful forms of recording in the early stages one must move on carefully to the introduction of the conventional forms of both vertical and horizontal computation. A child should be able to watch as a bundle of, say, ten rods and two extra ones are added to a set already containing a bundle of ten rods and three extra ones and then write the operation as $12 + 13 = 25$ or

$$\begin{array}{r} 12 \\ +13 \\ \hline 25 \end{array}$$

The reverse of this procedure is to show the child a 'number sentence' $(20 - 13 = 7)$ and ask him or her to demonstrate what this means using some form of concrete material. Dienes' MAB blocks are particularly useful for this purpose. Stern's equipment and Unifix blocks, being larger in size, are more appropriate for children with poor manipulative skills.

This stage of development is likely to require careful structuring over a long period of time if the slower learner is not to become confused. The grading of the examples and the amount of practice provided at each stage are crucial for long-term mastery. Once the children reach this stage of applying the basic algorithms for addition (with and without carrying), subtraction (with and without borrowing), multiplication and division, the demands on their thinking and reasoning increase rapidly (Beattie: 1986).

Skemp (1976) suggested that students should achieve two levels of understanding in their application of arithmetical processes to problem solving. The most basic level is termed *'instrumental understanding'* (knowing what to do and when to do it in order to select an appropriate process to solve a problem and then complete the calculation correctly). At this level the learner knows *what* to do but does not necessarily have an in-depth understanding of why or how the procedure works.

An example would be the application of the rule to invert and multiply when dividing by a fraction. The higher level of understanding is termed *'relational understanding.'* At this level the learner understands fully how and why a particular process works, as well as when to use it. Ideally one would hope to assist all children to achieve both levels of understanding; but realistically the relational level may be beyond the grasp of lower ability children. However it is possible to teach many of these children who have mastered the basic number system to select and carry out the correct arithmetical procedure to solve a problem. For everyday purposes that ability is all that is required.

Indirectly, the issues above raise the question of the place of the pocket calculator as a means of bypassing the computational difficulties of some students. There is a valid argument that time spent on mechanical arithmetic is largely wasted on a child who cannot seem to retain the steps involved in carrying out a particular procedure when working through a calculation using pencil and paper. The use of the calculator as a permanent alternative is totally defensible in such cases. As Beardslee (1978) has said, the use of the calculator removes a major obstacle for children with poor computational skills and they can all compute with speed and accuracy. The instructional time saved can then be devoted to helping the children learn to select the correct type of operation needed to solve particular problems: *more time on problem solving, not less!*

However, it is likely that in the foreseeable future many teachers will still wish to teach computational procedures in traditional written forms before a child is permitted to use a calculator. It is to these teachers that the following paragraphs in this section are directed.

What is the place of rote learning and the use of verbal cues for carrying out the steps in a particular calculation? For example, using the decomposition method for this subtraction problem the children would be taught to verbalise the steps in some way similar to the wording below.

$$5 \;_7\!\!\!\not{8} \; {}^1 1$$
$$-1 \;\; 3 \;\; 9$$
$$\overline{4 \;\; 4 \;\; 2}$$

The child says: 'Start with the units. I can't take 9 from 1 so I must borrow a ten and write it next to the 1. Cross out the 8 tens and write 7. Now I can take 9 from 11 and write 2 in the answer.

7 take 3 leaves 4 in the tens column. 5 take 1 leaves 4. Write 4 in the answer space. My answer is four hundred and forty-two.'

121

Such rote learning of these verbal routines has fallen into disrepute in recent years (Davis: 1984). It is felt that these methods inhibit the brighter children's thinking and may prevent them from devising insightful and more rapid methods of completing a calculation. Slavishly following an algorithm may represent purely mechanical performance even below the instrumental level. Nevertheless, for children with poor aptitude for arithmetic it is essential that, if the teacher does decide to cover these paper and pencil skills, they be taught thoroughly to the point of mastery. Without the verbal and mechanical procedures for working through a calculation the slower children are likely to be totally confused and utterly frustrated.

A remedial teacher who attempts to help a child in this area of school work *must* liaise closely with the class teacher in order to find out the precise verbal cues which are used in subtraction, multiplication, etc., so that the same words and directions are used in the remedial programme to avoid confusion.

---

*SELF-TESTING EXERCISE 7.2*

*The place of the pocket calculator in the mathematics course remains a vexed issue for many teachers. Set down your own views on the matter and address yourself particularly to its possible value for lower ability children. What are your views on the teaching of computational skills in fairly traditional ways involving set algorithms and verbal cueing?*

---

The increased interest in providing children with experience in manipulating sets has extended to more meaningful ways of teaching both addition and subtraction of hundreds, tens and units. For example, if the child is faced with 47 + 17 = he is encouraged to think of this (to regroup) as a set of (40 + 7) added to a set of (10 + 7). The tens are quickly combined to make 50, and the two 7's to make 14. Finally 14 combined with 50 is obviously 64. Fewer errors seem to occur with this method than with the 'carry the ten under the line' type of vertical addition. This is almost certainly because the approach is meaningful and does help to develop insight into the structure of number. It can also be easily demonstrated using MAB blocks or similar concrete materials (Suydam: 1986).

With subtraction the procedure may be illustrated thus:

(53 — 27 = )  53 can be regrouped as 40 + 13
27 can be regrouped as 20 + 7
Deal with the tens first: 40 — 20 = 20
Now the second step: 13 — 7 = 6
We are left with 26.

Once the method is established with relational understanding it appears to result in fewer errors than either 'decomposition' or 'equal addition' methods. Equal addition, once considered to be the best method for tackling more difficult subtraction problems, has fallen out of favour.

In the surveys which have been carried out to determine adult needs in arithmetic, multiplication and division do not appear to be of great value in everyday life. Certainly it is useful to be able to multiply, say, 23 lengths of wallpaper by 3 m to find out how much to order to paper a room; but the adult who has difficulty with multiplication will usually solve the problem correctly as an addition process (setting down 23 three times and adding). It seems that if teachers are to sort out the priorities for curriculum content in mathematics, addition and subtraction should be given high ranking, multiplication moderate ranking, and division low ranking. For children of limited ability a pocket calculator may well be the most obvious answer for multiplication and division.

One final word on the paper and pencil performance of children with perceptual difficulties or co-ordination problems. It is often necessary to rule up the pages of their exercise books in ways which will make it easier for them to set down the digits in correct spatial positions. Heavy vertical lines will assist with the correct placement of H, T and U and thus maintain place values. Squared paper will usually assist with the general arrangement of figures on the page. Teachers must also anticipate the difficulties which some children will have in reversing not only single digits but tens and units (e.g. 61 written as 16). Much specific teaching, with cues and prompts such as small arrows or dots on the page, will be needed to overcome this tendency.

### Mental Arithmetic: Does it still have a place?

Mental arithmetic — the 'daily ten' — has an almost sacred position in the primary mathematics lesson. If the activity is used to review and practise important skills or facts and *if there is corrective feedback* provided for the children who make

123

errors, then the time is well spent. However, in many classrooms the session really is nothing more than a ritual if the questions are posed, the answers given and a mark given out of ten with no follow-up whatsoever for children with poor scores. The teacher must identify which questions caused difficulty and spend a few moments reteaching the necessary procedure to solve the problems.

One simple teaching strategy which is extremely helpful for children who are poor at processing purely auditory information is to write the numerals on the blackboard as the problem is posed orally. For example, the teacher says, 'Red team scored 9 goals. Blue team scored 7 goals. Green team scored 12 goals. How many goals scored altogether?' The numerals 9, 7 and 12 are quickly written randomly on the blackboard. Having this key information available in visual form will enable many more children to add the numbers mentally.

It is worth commenting that hearing-impaired children may have particular difficulties with mental arithmetic when the questions are dictated by the teacher. A number such as 'sixty' may *look* exactly like 'sixteen' on the teacher's lips if the child relies heavily on speech reading. Again the use of blackboard will help to prevent this confusion.

### Developing Problem Solving Strategies

In an article *'You can teach problem solving'* LeBlanc (1977) stated optimistically, 'Teaching problem solving is a problem; but like most other problems it can be solved' (p.16). He then went on to present a framework to help children develop problem solving skills. His ideas, together with those of Riley and Pachtman (1978) and Darch, Carnine and Gersten (1984) have been summarised in the following paragraphs. The instructional goal should be to help children learn strategies and procedures for problem solving. They need to learn how to approach a problem without a feeling of panic or hopelessness. They need to be able to sift the relevant from the irrelevant information and impose some degree of structure on the problem (Carpenter: 1985).

Take the example, *A store sold 485 bottles of cold drink on one day in the summer. The drink bottles are packaged in cartons which hold 6 bottles each. How many cartons of drink were sold that day?*

Step 1: *Understanding the problem*

The teacher focuses the children's attention on the relevant information in the problem through the use of questions.

'How many bottles were sold?'

'What does packaged mean?' 'What is a carton?' (Visual aid or blackboard sketch may be helpful even at this stage.)

'How were the bottles packed?'

'If one carton holds six bottles how many bottles in 2 cartons?'

'How many bottles in 10 cartons?'

'What does the problem ask us to find out?'

**N.B.** Advice such as *'think!'* or *'read it again!'* may be of no help to the child.

Step 2: *Planning to solve the problem*

The teacher encourages the child or children to consider possible ways of solving the problem. If necessary the teacher may need to offer some suggestions. 'Well, could we do it like this? Could we get 485 bottles and put them into groups of six? Do we need to do that? How else could we do it? Could we make up some form of chart or table? Will a sketch help us to visualise what to do? Both Macdonald (1975) and Nelson (1983) stress the immense value of having children *draw sketches* which help them to picture the actual problem.

Step 3: *Attempting a solution*

The children might now attempt, perhaps through trial and error to some extent, to come up with a plausible answer.

Step 4: *Reviewing the problem and its solution*

In this final stage the children are encouraged to consider the problem again and to check to see if their solution is what was asked for. 'John, you've got 2910 cartons. Does that make sense?' 'Why?' 'Tell us how you got that?' 'Linda, you have written *80 and a bit cartons;* tell us how you got that.'

LeBlanc suggests that this final stage in teaching problem solving is very important indeed. It benefits the child who is having to think carefully *how* he solved the problem and it is helping the other children who hear (in language they can readily understand) how someone else tackled the problem.

125

Riley & Pachtman (1978) consider that the most important thing to teach is how to sift out the key information from the facts which are presented. The children must be helped to perceive the relationships between the statements in the problem and to detect the relevant facts. This is basically a reading comprehension problem. Darch, Carnine & Gersten (1984) developed a four-step programme for aiding this process. The children are taught (i) to write down the numbers from the problem (ii) to identify the process needed to work with the numbers (iii) to write the equation or algorithm (iv) to write the solution. The teacher models these steps very carefully and directly instructs the children in their use. They found significant improvement in fourth grade children's problem solving skills following this type of training. Similar improvement has been found with adolescents (Montague & Candace: 1986).

Since there is evidence that children can be helped to become more proficient in solving problems teachers of children with learning difficulties should devote more time to this area of work. As mentioned in an earlier section, perhaps the use of pocket calculators will enable teachers to find the time to do this rather than to restrict the children to a diet of mechanical arithmetic (Burns: 1986).

---

### SELF-TESTING EXERCISE 7.3

*Briefly outline some strategies you would use to help some slower learning children solve this problem.*
*'At the beginning of the new term Class 7, with 25 children in it, has been given a collection of 98 books to increase the size of their classroom library. Before the holiday they had 102 books in the library. The teacher says, "I want labels pasted in all the books, new and old. You can share the work out equally so that you all have a turn at pasting".*
*If the work is divided up fairly, in how many books will each child have to paste labels?'*

---

## Curriculum Content

With slow learning and disabled children it is frequently necessary to modify somewhat the actual content which one attempts to cover. Some traditional topics in mainstream mathematics courses are inappropriate for these children. Cockcroft (1982) supports the notion of a reduced-content maths course with a *functional* emphasis for children of limited ability. In trying to decide upon content for a 'Core Curriculum' one is helped by the results of surveys of community expectations of basic numeracy (Bourke: 1981). Parents and employers agree that the key areas for functional numeracy are: counting, tables, use of the four basic processes, money management, time and measurement. Some grasp of common and decimal fractions and the ability to understand simple graphs are also useful in everyday life.

The following content was considered by a group of primary and secondary teachers to comprise a core of essential material basic to the needs of low achieving school-leavers. Items marked with an asterisk could be omitted with children of low ability. (See also the even more limited content of Fredericks et al curriculum for the moderately to severely handicapped which follows this.)

## Suggested core content

### Basic number

- ☐ Digit (numeral) recognition. Ability to count actual objects correctly. Understanding of cardinal and serial aspects of number. Appreciation of place value. Emphasis on establishing basic number facts as *habit responses*.
- ☐ Standard processes (algorithms) of arithmetic. Emphasis on addition, subtraction. Emphasis on 'estimating' reasonable results for calculations. Greatest emphasis on *problem solving* using basic processes.
- ☐ Multiplication and division to be taught later using realistic numbers. Grouping. (No objection to table charts or desk calculators.) Counting in intervals (2's, 5's, 10's, 100's).

### Money

- ☐ Coin and note recognition.
- ☐ Ability to handle money (count up totals using the coins; give change by 'counting-on' method).
- ☐ Ability to perform basic processes with $ and cents, £ and p (esp. + and —).
- ☐ Experiences with simple budgeting and banking.

### Problem solving

- ☐ Emphasis to be placed on applying all the above skills and processes to solving problems.
- ☐ Emphasis also on *practical* mathematics.
- ☐ Use of measurement scale in simple mapwork and interpretation.*
- ☐ Ability to interpret simple graphs and charts.*

127

*Fractions, decimals, percentages*
- [ ] Understanding and recognition of simple common fractions (½, ¾, ¼, ⅒). No *rote learning* of operations with fractions. Equivalence of simple fractions.
- [ ] Understanding and recognition of tenths and hundredths and decimal notation, particularly in connection with measurement (linear, temperature, etc.) and money.*
- [ ] Awareness of the meaning of 100%, 50%, 25%, 10%, with particular reference to Sales and '10% off', etc.*

*Measurement*
- [ ] Ability to measure and construct using mm, cm and metres. Awareness of distance (km). Speed (km/hr) (and associated road signs).*
- [ ] Ability to weigh in gms and kgms. Awareness of common weights of goods (e.g. packet of sugar, potatoes, etc.). Basic understanding of tonne.*
- [ ] Ability to tell the time. Probably best to teach digital clock notation (rather than '¼ past', '¼ to', etc.). Teach that clock face is really a curved number line 1 to 60. Awareness of the passage of time (e.g. 30 seconds; 1 minute; 5 minutes; 1 hour; 24 hours). Estimate 'how long will it take?' — to do a certain task, or to travel a certain journey, or to get to the bus stop, etc.).
- [ ] Know days of the week, months of the year, and seasons.
- [ ] Liquid measures (litre). Relate to petrol, cans of paint, carton of milk or juice, etc.*
- [ ] Temperature. Read thermometer.*

**A Suggested Core for Moderately to Severely Handicapped Children**

Adapted from Fredericks (1976) and Bender et al (1976).

*Number concepts*
The child:
 Rote counts to ten
 Counts objects to ten
 Gives correct number of objects (up to ten) on request
 Matches numerals one to ten
 Counts and points to numerals one to ten in sequence
 Finds correct numeral on request
 Names numerals to ten (any order) when shown card
 Matches numerals to groups (up to ten)
 Rote counts to twenty
 Copies numerals one to ten

Writes numeral from dictation
Adds with objects to ten (combines groups)
Counts objects to twenty
Adds with numbers to ten
Subtracts with objects to ten
Subtracts with numbers to ten
Combines objects to twenty
Rote counts to one hundred

*Monetary concepts*
Matches coins and notes
Identifies coins and notes on request
Knows value of coins and notes

*Concepts of telling time*
Says days of week by rote
Says months of year by rote
Correlates general times of day
Tells time (digital clock)

*Personal information concepts*
Gives parents' full names
Gives birthdate
Names self as male or female
Gives address
Gives own telephone number
Dials phone number

## One Minute Basic Number Facts Tests

These instructions must be followed carefully if use is to be made of the norms provided in Tables A and B.

It is permissible to write the test items out using numerals of a larger size and allowing more space for answers to be written. The child must write the answers on the test slip next to the question, not waste time transferring them to a separate sheet.

Give out the test slips for the addition facts first, placing each slip face down on the child's desk. The child writes his/her name on the back. Later the teacher will write the child's age to nearest half-year from school records.

*Say:* 'When you turn the sheet over you will find some *addition* sums. I want you to write down the answer to each one as quickly as you can on the slip of paper. Write it next to the sum. When I say START, work

129

quickly until I say STOP. Do as many as you can but don't worry if you don't finish them all.
Pencils ready. START NOW.'

After exactly one minute say: 'STOP. Pencils down.' Make sure that every child stops at once. Collect the papers for marking.

Give out the subtraction slips and follow the above instructions, substituting the words *subtraction (take away)* for the word addition. *Remind the children twice* that they are to subtract this time.

It is advisable that if the multiplication facts and division facts are to be tested this should be done after a short break; for example, after recess in the morning.

The tests were normed by Westwood et al (1974) in England and by Broughton (1975) in Australia. No significant difference in performance was found between the two populations.

The test-retest reliability is between .92 and .89.

The tests may be reproduced without infringing copyright.

### Norms for the number facts tests

**Note:** The 'critically low score' is the score which places the child in the bottom 10% of children in that age range. It can be taken as a clear sign that the child requires more than the ordinary amount of time devoted to improving recall of number facts.

*TABLE A*

*Addition*

| Age (yrs) | 5½ | 6 | 6½ | 7 | 7½ | 8 | 8½ | 9 | 9½ | 10 | 10½ | 11 |
|---|---|---|---|---|---|---|---|---|---|---|---|---|
| Mean Score | 2.5 | 4.5 | 7 | 10 | 13.5 | 15.5 | 17.5 | 19 | 20 | 21 | 22 | 23 |
| Critically Low Score | 0 | 2 | 3 | 6 | 7 | 9 | 12 | 13 | 14 | 15 | 15 | 16 |

*Subtraction*

| Age (yrs) | 5½ | 6 | 6½ | 7 | 7½ | 8 | 8½ | 9 | 9½ | 10 | 10½ | 11 |
|---|---|---|---|---|---|---|---|---|---|---|---|---|
| Mean Score | 1 | 3.5 | 6.5 | 8.5 | 10.5 | 12 | 13 | 15 | 16.5 | 17.5 | 19 | 21 |
| Critically Low Score | 0 | 0 | 3 | 6 | 8 | 9 | 10 | 11 | 12 | 13 | 13 | 14 |

## TABLE B
### Multiplication

| Age (yrs) | 8½ | 9 | 9½ | 10 | 10½ | 11 | 11½ | 12 | 12½ |
|---|---|---|---|---|---|---|---|---|---|
| Mean Score | 12.5 | 12.5 | 15 | 17 | 20 | 22 | 23.5 | 25 | 26.5 |
| Critically Low Score | 7 | 7 | 9 | 11 | 13 | 15 | 17 | 18 | 21 |

### Division

| Age (yrs) | 8½ | 9 | 9½ | 10 | 10½ | 11 | 11½ | 12 | 12½ |
|---|---|---|---|---|---|---|---|---|---|
| Mean Score | 7.5 | 8 | 10 | 13 | 13.5 | 15.5 | 18 | 20 | 21.5 |
| Critically Low Score | 3 | 3 | 4 | 6 | 7 | 8 | 10 | 11 | 14 |

## One Minute Basic Number Facts Tests

| Addition | Subtraction | Multiplication | Division |
|---|---|---|---|
| 2 + 1 = | 2 − 1 = | 1 × 2 = | 2 ÷ 1 = |
| 1 + 4 = | 5 − 1 − | 2 × 3 = | 4 ÷ 2 = |
| 2 + 2 = | 3 − 2 = | 2 × 5 = | 3 ÷ 1 = |
| 4 + 2 = | 5 − 3 = | 1 × 4 = | 6 ÷ 3 = |
| 3 + 4 = | 6 − 2 = | 3 × 2 = | 8 ÷ 2 = |
| 2 + 3 = | 2 − 2 = | 4 × 3 = | 9 ÷ 3 = |
| 5 + 2 = | 6 − 4 = | 9 × 1 = | 10 ÷ 2 = |
| 4 + 5 = | 7 − 2 = | 6 × 2 = | 12 ÷ 3 = |
| 3 + 5 = | 6 − 1 = | 3 × 4 = | 15 ÷ 5 = |
| 2 + 8 = | 7 − 3 = | 5 × 3 = | 16 ÷ 4 = |
| 4 + 4 = | 8 − 2 = | 7 × 2 = | 18 ÷ 3 = |
| 2 + 5 = | 7 − 5 = | 3 × 6 = | 20 ÷ 4 = |
| 1 + 8 = | 8 − 3 = | 2 × 8 = | 21 ÷ 3 = |
| 6 + 4 = | 7 − 4 = | 4 × 5 = | 24 ÷ 4 = |
| 3 + 7 = | 9 − 3 = | 9 × 2 = | 30 ÷ 3 = |
| 6 + 3 = | 8 − 5 = | 3 × 7 = | 30 ÷ 5 = |
| 5 + 5 = | 9 − 5 = | 6 × 4 = | 24 ÷ 8 = |
| 6 + 2 = | 10 − 4 = | 3 × 9 = | 27 ÷ 3 = |
| 2 + 7 = | 9 − 4 = | 8 × 3 = | 50 ÷ 5 = |
| 4 + 6 = | 10 − 3 = | 7 × 0 − | 28 ÷ 4 = |
| 5 + 7 − | 11 − 2 = | 8 × 4 = | 32 ÷ 8 = |
| 8 + 3 = | 10 − 6 = | 5 × 6 = | 35 ÷ 5 = |
| 4 + 9 = | 12 − 3 = | 4 × 7 = | 42 ÷ 6 = |
| 7 + 6 = | 12 − 6 = | 8 × 6 = | 45 ÷ 5 = |
| 8 + 6 = | 11 − 5 = | 7 × 5 = | 48 ÷ 8 = |
| 9 + 8 = | 13 − 3 = | 9 × 4 = | 54 ÷ 6 = |
| 6 + 9 = | 12 − 9 = | 8 × 9 = | 36 ÷ 9 = |
| 8 + 7 = | 14 − 6 = | 7 × 7 = | 56 ÷ 7 = |
| 9 + 5 = | 17 − 8 = | 6 × 9 = | 64 ÷ 8 = |
| 9 + 7 = | 16 − 9 = | 8 × 8 = | 63 : 9 − |
| 9 + 3 = | 18 − 9 = | 6 × 8 = | 72 ÷ 8 = |
| 8 + 4 = | 17 − 6 = | 9 × 9 = | 81 ÷ 9 = |
| 8 + 8 = | 16 − 8 = | 9 × 7 = | 88 ÷ 8 = |

131

## Summary

In this chapter brief attention was given to factors which may cause children to experience difficulty learning basic mathematics.

Three levels of diagnostic assessment were presented. A teacher using the items listed at each level should obtain a fairly accurate picture of what a child can and cannot do in number work and simple problem solving.

Priority attention was given to practical ways of helping a child develop number fluency since this is basic to all problem solving work. It was suggested that for some students a pocket calculator be provided as a permanent alternative to paper and pencil computation.

Suggestions were provided for the teaching of problem solving skills through modelling appropriate step-by-step procedures.

Finally, suggested 'core curriculum in mathematics' was presented first for slower and mildly handicapped students and then for the moderately to severely handicapped students.

**Further Reading**

Ashlock, R. B., Johnson, M. L., Wilson, J. W. & Jones, W. (1983) *Guiding each child's learning in mathematics.* Columbus, Merrill.

Bley, N. S. & Thornton, C. A. (1981) *Teaching mathematics to the learning disabled.* Rockville, Aspen.

Burton, G. M. (1985) *Towards a good beginning: teaching early childhood mathematics.* Menlo Park, Addison-Wesley.

Cornelius, M. (1982) *Teaching mathematics.* London, Croom Helm.

Davis, R. B. (1984) *Learning mathematics.* London, Croom Helm.

Ginsburg, H. (1982) *Children's arithmetic; how they learn it and how you teach it.* Austin, Pro-Ed.

Gullatt, D. E. (1986) Help your students read mathematics. *Arithmetic Teacher* 33 (9): 20-21.

Hembree, R. (1986) Effects of hand-held calculators in pre-college mathematics education. *Journal of Research in Mathematics Education* 17 (2): 83-99.

Silbert, J., Carnine, D. & Stein, M. (1981) *Direct instruction mathematics.* Columbus, Merrill.

Suydam, M. N. & Reys, R. E. (1978) *Developing computational skills.* Reston, National Council of Teachers of Mathematics.

# 8 SCHOOL-BASED AND REGIONAL SUPPORT SYSTEMS

*'Our work has convinced us that much is to be gained by further developing and extending our supportive role in preference to continuing to function within a system of extraction. Indeed, not only can a system of in-class support benefit special needs pupils and those who teach them, it can also have far reaching effects on many of the integral components of the whole school.'* (Lavers, Pickup & Thomson: 1986, p.34)

## Introduction

This final chapter looks briefly at the issues involved in providing support for children with special needs and for the regular class teachers who work with them. When the integration of handicapped children was first undertaken in earnest in America, Australia and Britain it was always agreed that an effective support system would be crucial for the success of the venture. Unfortunately, in all three countries the amount of support available to a school or to a particular teacher is not always adequate. Many teachers with handicapped children in their classes are left to work out their own salvation. Large schools, particularly those in metropolitan areas, may be able to justify extra staff and will have easy access to any centralised support service. The small schools, particularly in isolated rural areas, experience the greatest difficulty in receiving regular and effective help.

Even when a support service is available there may be problems involved in its staffing or its operation (Kokaska: 1985). Very special skills are needed by teachers who are going to advise others and those skills are not always present in the staff appointed to support or resource roles. In the final part of this chapter the problems and practices of resource teaching are discussed. First it will be useful to consider what a school can do to help itself cope with children demanding more than the ordinary amount of assistance.

## Helping Strategies within the Classroom

One of the major problems faced by the teacher who is willing to accept a handicapped child into the regular class is how to organise in such a way that, if necessary, he or she can spend a little time with that child each day. This individual attention must not be achieved at the expense of other children in the group. The following options are worth consideration.

133

## Peer and Cross-age Group Tutoring

Bloom (1978), in a book dealing with peer-group and cross-age tutoring, describes the creation of a system whereby students can help each other to learn. This should not always be seen as 'the more able helping the less able' but rather students working in the role of tutor and tutee and applying the principle 'One who teaches also learns'.

All the advocates of peer-group or cross-age tutoring stress the importance of having preparation sessions for the tutors so that they may adopt appropriate skills and techniques. Bloom has written, *In my own work in training tutors for peer tutoring at the elementary school level, I have found that the tutors need:*

*(a) Clear directions as to what they are to do and how they are to do it.*

*(b) A specific learning task and specific instructional materials for that task.*

*(c) A model of appropriate tutoring behaviours for the task.*

*(d) An opportunity to role play or practise with feedback and correction and, possibly, a second opportunity to review the model and practise further.*

*(e) Some opportunity to make a choice of materials or games and even the possibility of creating or reinterpreting learning materials.*

*To meet these conditions, where the student tutor has already learned the content to be taught, only a short training period is necessary' (p.11).*

Peer-group tutoring at various ability levels has the advantage of reducing the time a teacher needs to spend interacting with a whole class. It thus increases the amount of time he or she has to work directly with students who have learning problems. Alternatively, a child with a problem, for example in mathematics, reading or writing, may well be helped very efficiently by a friend in the class or by a child from a higher grade. Many schools make use of older children to help younger children, to the benefit of both. It appears that the 'tutors' use simple, direct language and demonstrate more rapidly and effectively what is required than do many teachers!

## Teacher aides and para-professionals

An aide can either work individually with the child on material and activities planned by the teacher, or the aide could supervise in a general way the rest of the class on work set by the teacher while the teacher works with the child. The aide should not be expected to determine what the child needs, that is clearly the teacher's responsibility.

Aides can fulfil the role of 'trusted adults' who have time to listen to individual children's interests and worries. They are therefore instrumental in improving the child's communication skills while acting as counsellor and friend.

## Parents

Many schools now involve parents (not necessarily the parent of the handicapped child) in the educational programme. They usually require some degree of training or preparation by the teacher in order to be used to maximum advantage (e.g. how to listen to a child read; how to talk with children; how to operate a particular word-building or number game; etc.). The suggested training to be given to peer tutors described above might apply equally to parent helpers.

## Volunteer helpers

They are often used to excellent advantage in special schools. With unemployment running at a high level many volunteers could be found for work in ordinary schools. Some retired people who wish to remain active have been used very successfully as tutors in high school programmes and as mentors in gifted children's projects. The preparation they need is similar to that described for peer tutors.

## High School and College students

Many high school students are gaining experience from working with children in kindergartens and junior primary schools. This is usually as part of a work-experience or community-involvement programme for senior students. If their presence is time tabled on a regular basis the teacher can make use of their services for group work or individual help.

## Team Teaching

If two or more teachers are prepared to work together for at least part of each day, the organisational options are at once increased. Quite large groups may be taken for certain activities (e.g. films, TV, story, etc.) by one teacher, so releasing the other/s to work with quite small groups or individuals.

## Principal or Deputy

The head teacher or deputy may take a regular time slot with the class thus releasing the teacher for individual work with certain children.

*Support Teachers*

Usually if a child with special needs is to be integrated into the class the services of a special education support teacher will be provided for at least a few hours a week. Some aspects of this support service have already been mentioned above, others are dealt with in more detail later in the chapter.

## What do Regular Class Teachers Need to Know?

The teacher with a handicapped child in his or her class needs to know:

- [ ] how to establish specific objectives for the child in both the academic and the social areas; and how to use these objectives as the basis for regular assessment of progress;
- [ ] how to teach diagnostically and adapt teaching procedures to match the characteristics and needs of the child;
- [ ] how to provide learning situations which will enable the handicapped child to be 'counted in' as much as possible with the other children and make a contribution to the lessons *(instructional integration);*
- [ ] how to create situations where social skills and group-working skills are developed through interaction between handicapped child and the peer group *(social integration);*
- [ ] how to plan and implement individual assignments or tasks if these are necessary for the child in order to provide training to overcome specific areas of weakness *(individual programming);*
- [ ] how to train a child in self-management skills and how to encourage independence and initiative;
- [ ] how to liaise effectively with parents in order to establish a situation of mutual trust and mutual help;
- [ ] how to liaise with specialists where necessary (e.g. speech therapist; psychologist);
- [ ] how to make optimum use of available support (both material and personnel);
- [ ] how to apply the strategies and tactics which are associated with high quality education for all children.

Hegarty (1982) has commented, *'Particular care must be taken with monitoring pupils' progress and ensuring that their overall programme is balanced'* (p.102). 'Balance' in this context involves all of the following:

- [ ] sufficient individual programming to ensure academic progress and at least some remediation of specific weaknesses;

☐ sufficient group activities to foster social development and acceptance;
☐ sufficient guidance to provide help for the child without maintaining his or her dependence;
☐ sufficient opportunity for the child to show initiative, develop self-management skills and discover areas of strength and interest.

## The Resource Room Model

Children who have been mainstreamed may still need to receive additional help from personnel outside the classroom setting. The resource room model as a school-based support system has gained in popularity in the last few years. Sceptics will argue that it is nothing more than the old 'remedial withdrawal room' given a more palatable name. Advocates will point out that the resource room operates in a much more flexible manner than the traditional remedial room and provides a base from which the support or resource teacher can operate. Children may go to the room for special help but it is equally likely that the teacher may go to the child's classroom to provide the needed help. The resource room is also seen as the collecting house for materials and ideas which can be shared among the school staff when appropriate. It may also provide a focal point in the school for materials and ideas for the *most able* as well as the least able students.

Resource room programming may involve the resource teacher in setting up such strategies as peer-group or cross-age group tutoring in specific classes. Resource teachers an produce greater impact when they manage a support syste n involving other personnel than when they merely instruct small groups or individuals themselves.

In some of the American literature dealing with resource rooms it is quite clear that in certain schools they do function much as a traditional remedial centre and cater mainly for children with reading problems. For that reason they must be open to the same doubts in terms of long-term benefits which have plagued remedial programmes, i.e. that the children make gains while in the programme but fail to maintain these, or even regress, as soon as the extra help is withdrawn. Doubts have been voiced about the overall success of resource room programming. The problem appears to be that much of the individualised special help given in the resource room does not transfer to the regular classroom since the learning environment there remains unchanged. Demands in the regular classroom may still be too great for the particular child's existing skills so that for every half-hour spent in the resource room in a success situation five hours may be spent failing in the regular class. This is why there has been a shift towards providing support for the children within the regular class situation (Lavers, Pickup & Thomson: 1986).

Sindelar & Deno (1978) reviewed seventeen studies concerned with the efficacy of resource programming. They conclude that in the academic domain, learning disabled and mildly disturbed children seem to benefit more than retarded children from resource room programmes. In the personal-social domain positive effects of resource programming have yet to be established.

### The Role of the Resource (Support) Teacher

The support teacher is in the school to provide a service to children with special needs by assisting the classroom teacher develop or adapt appropriate learning programmes to cater for exceptional children. He or she may spend time teaching children individually or in small groups within the classroom or in withdrawal situations. The support teacher works in co-operation with the class teacher and his or her work should supplement the regular class teacher's programme, not replace it.

Bearing in mind that teachers and principals consider that the support teacher should spend not less than 50% of his or her time in direct teaching of children, the following duties are usually seen as part of the support teacher's role.

☐ Educational assessment and diagnosis using formal and informal methods in conjunction with information provided by specialists or agencies.

☐ Collating and disseminating such information.

☐ Regular discussion with class teachers about suitable educational programmes and activities for children with special needs.

☐ The provision or loan of resource materials to assist with the teaching of specific skills or concepts where necessary.

☐ Regular evaluation of the progress made by children receiving direct support; and the keeping of appropriate records.

☐ Teaching of individuals or small groups within the classroom or elsewhere.

☐ Team teaching with the regular class teacher.
☐ Taking the class while the class teacher works with a small group.
☐ Providing some school-based inservice staff development seminars.

If support teachers are working across several schools in a region they should be deployed in such a way that they do not have too many schools or too many children to service. Efficiency will be lessened if the service is spread too thinly. It is best that a thorough job be done intensively in a small number of schools or with a small number of students for a viable period. As class teachers become more adaptive in their approach to children with special needs it should be possible to withdraw much of the direct help which was required initially.

## What Do Support Teachers Need To Know?

Regardless of whether a special education teacher provides help to a regular class teacher via a resource room programme, team teaching, through advice or through any combination of these, certain issues are important. Little (1978) has highlighted the vital importance of support and resource teachers having what he calls 'change-agent skills'. They need to be able to relate appropriately to the teachers with whom they work and consult and with school principals who may be the key individuals in agreeing or not agreeing to vary organisational patterns, provide particular materials, set up and support specific programmes. The 'change-agent/support teacher' role is a very difficult one. To be able to relate to and influence the behaviour of colleagues requires enormous tact and subtlety. One of the most obvious temptations for the support teacher to avoid is 'coming the expert'. The 'I-know-all-there-is-to-know-about-the-things-you-don't-understand-or-can't-cope-with' attitude will *not* establish the necessary helping relationship through mutual trust. From the first moment of contact with a teacher who has requested advice or help the support teacher should establish the idea that he or she is there to work out possible solutions or strategies jointly, that there are no ready-made answers or panaceas but that *together* they will try various solutions.

It is vital that the support teacher recognises from the start that a teacher who seeks help has certain attitudes and expectations concerning the child referred for special help.

139

These attitudes and expectations may be very positive and very realistic or they may be totally unrealistic. That teacher will also have certain expectations of the support teacher which may be unrealistic. Whatever the attitude and expectations are they will not be changed overnight. Establishing a working relationship with the teacher should be seen as a process of mutual adaptation. The support teacher will have to adapt quite as much to the teacher's current knowledge, style and skills as he or she will have to adapt any suggestion the support teacher makes.

The following lists of 'Do's and Don'ts' may provide at least a basic introduction to support work and highlight the interpersonal relationship factors inevitably involved in providing help or bringing about change. Several of these points are obviously more applicable to the visiting support teacher rather than the school-based teacher.

### Some Do's for the Support Teacher

☐ *Do be a good listener.* Clearly indicate that you are genuinely interested in all that the teacher wants to tell you (even if you don't, at the time, agree with some of what is said). Your role as a listener will be conveyed more by non-verbal cues than by anything you say. Such things as eye contact, facial expression, physical stance and proximity to the speaker are all important. To get others to talk you need to talk less yourself and to ask open-ended questions which invite longer answers.

☐ *Do seek information which is to the point.* For example, ask to see examples of a child's work or school report. Discuss these. Ask for more detail about some of what is said (e.g. if the teacher has described some incidents of bad behaviour ask if he/she knows what triggers them off, do they happen at the same time of day, or in the same type of lesson, or the same type of classroom grouping? etc.).

☐ *Do find something in the classroom and/or lesson to praise.* Be precise in your reasons for praising it.

☐ *Do stress the need to 'collaborate' with the teacher.* Agree from the start that you will work together to find solutions to the problems. Do not give the impression that you can work miracles.

140

☐ *Do try to 'read between the lines'.* Ask yourself, 'Is this teacher really asking for help and advice or hoping that I will confirm that there is nothing anyone can do?' 'Where is this teacher's locus of control? Does the teacher really think that there is anything he/she can do to change the situation; or does she really believe that the child's difficulties are determined by factors beyond his/her control?'

☐ *Do bring the conversation around to focus on some attainable, short-term goal which you can both work towards during the coming week.* It is helpful to set down some short-term objectives. Get the teacher to do something between your first and second visit. Perhaps get them to note more systematically when certain behaviours occur; or note more precisely what causes a child to produce such a small amount of written work in a given period; or determine precisely what phonic knowledge the child does have. You may be able to leave checklists for the teacher to use, but make these fairly simple and quick to apply. If some ideas occur to you during your visit make some suggestions but do not guarantee success and do not over-load the teacher.

☐ *Do observe the child in various situations and try to spend some time working with him or her even on the first visit.*

☐ *Do allow the teacher to see what you are doing with the child when you work with him or her.* This should not be in the form of a 'demonstration'; merely approach the task in a very open manner which enables the teacher to notice any particular strategies you use.

☐ *Do bring suitable resource materials and leave these with the teacher.* However, avoid giving the impression that kits and games or worksheets are going to provide the answer to all the problems. Select your materials carefully: if they are too simple or too difficult and the child does not like them, the result will undermine your credibility.

☐ *Do work in close co-operation with other specialist personnel (e.g. educational psychologist, play therapist).*

☐ *Do suggest the need for reassessment if you think that the child is not coping adequately,* even with the extra support. The class teacher may feel reluctant to do this as he or she may feel that it will reflect some degree of incompetence.

## Some Don'ts for the Support Teacher

☐ *Don't promise regular visiting services unless you are certain that you can provide these.*

☐ *Don't bite off more than you can chew in terms of programme planning and the provision of resources.*

☐ *Don't give the impression that certain methods or materials are infallible.* If they fail your credibility will be questioned and/or the teacher's confidence will be undermined.

☐ *Don't give the impression that you are pushed for time and must dash off to the next school.* Don't keep looking at your watch!

☐ *Don't gloss over the amount of time and effort that may be needed* if a certain approach is to be introduced. If the time involved is not feasible look for other alternatives.

☐ *Don't openly criticise a teacher's way of working, organising the classroom and dealing with difficulties.* If change is necessary it will need to be brought about by more subtle means.

☐ *Don't appear to be a mere courier of materials and resources.* Your colleagues may consider that you are too highly paid to act as a full-time delivery agent.

☐ *Don't fail to turn up at the school at the appointed time.* If you are unavoidably delayed, telephone the principal, explain the problem and arrange an alternative time.

## Conclusion

The mainstreaming of handicapped children is now an established practice. There is growing awareness of the factors which are important for its success in individual cases. Education authorities in general, and individual teachers in particular, must act responsibly in ensuring that the placement of a handicapped child is carefully monitored at regular intervals. If the placement is not proving to be satisfactory some modification must be made to the classroom situation or to the nature of the support services available in order to bring about an improvement. In some cases it may be in the child's interests to place him or her in a segregated setting, full-time or part-time, until the necessary changes in the child or the situation have been achieved. Placing a child in the mainstream should not be an irreversible decision.

SELF-TESTING EXERCISE 8.1

Your school probably has a significant number of children
with special educational needs. How might you determine
the size of the problem in your school?

Given an ideal situation how would you organise the time
table and deploy teaching staff and other available
personnel to create a viable support system?

Identify and list the main obstacles which would need to
be overcome in order to implement such a programme in
your school.

If your school already has a support system established
for children with special needs evaluate its present positive
and negative features. How might it be improved?

## Further Reading

Brennan, W. K. (1985) *Curriculum for special needs.* Milton
Keynes, Open University Press.

Clunies-Ross, L. (1984) Support the mainstream teacher. *Special
Education: Forward Trends* 11 (3): 9-11.

Davis, W. E. (1983) Competencies and skills needed to be an
effective resource teacher. *Journal of Learning Disabilities*
16 (10): 596-598.

Delquadri, J. et al (1986) Classwide peer tutoring. *Exceptional
Children* 52 (6): 535-542.

Haight, S. L. (1984) Special education consultant: idealism
versus realism. *Exceptional Children* 50 (6): 507-515.

Haynes, M. V. & Jenkins, J. R. (1986) Reading instruction in
special education resource rooms. *American Educational
Research Journal* Vol. 23 (2): 161-190.

Hockley, L. (1985) On being a support teacher. *British Journal
of Special Education* 12 (1): 27-29.

Sewell, G. (1982) *Reshaping remedial education.* London,
Croom Helm.

Smith, C. J. (1982) Helping colleagues cope: a consultant role
for the remedial teacher. *Remedial Education* 17 (2): 75-78.

Wiederholt, J. L., Hammill, D. D. & Brown, C. L. (1983) *The
resource teacher (2nd ed).* Austin, Pro-Ed.

## Application

*If you are appointed as a support teacher in a primary or secondary school, you may be asked for advice on the following issues.*

☐ *The main problems faced by a hearing impaired child in a regular classroom.*

☐ *The specific difficulties encountered by dyslexic students when attempting to use textbooks.*

☐ *The strategies which might be necessary when integrating a visually impaired child into a regular class.*

☐ *Modifications which might be necessary to the structural aspects of the school building and the classroom if a child in a wheelchair is to be accommodated successfully.*

*Be prepared to present your views on these issues at a staff seminar.*

*Some of your information can be obtained from books; but try also to discuss the particular issues with appropriate experts in the field.*

# POSTSCRIPTUM

It was suggested at the beginning of this book that there is really not very much that is 'special' about special education. In general this text has been about *effective teaching* as a means of reducing the prevalence of learning failure. It has also addressed the issue of catering for a wide ability range in any class.

McCormick (1979) identified a number of characteristics of teachers who helped children to achieve at better-than-expected levels. His summary provides a fitting conclusion to a book which has stressed *good commonsense* as the key ingredient in meeting the needs of children with and without disabilities and handicaps.

In schools where students achieve better results than expected teachers demonstrated a greater understanding of the structure and substance of the content being taught. In particular they:
- [ ] were more specific about lesson objectives;
- [ ] were better able to judge accurately the time needed to accomplish these objectives;
- [ ] made more frequent use of structuring comments as instruction proceeded;
- [ ] successfully broke the lessons into manageable and logical sequences;
- [ ] more ably anticipated problems in reaching the objectives and made accommodations for them.

Teachers also demonstrated a greater understanding of the special characteristics of their students. In particular they:
- [ ] more often modified instruction on the basis of student responses;
- [ ] used a vocabulary, oral and written, more appropriate for the age or ability level;
- [ ] adjusted the level of questions for different ability levels in the class;
- [ ] presented material at an appropriate level of difficulty.

Futhermore, the teachers demonstrated a greater understanding of the principles of learning. They:
- [ ] made frequent use of opportunities to create and maintain an appropriate mind-set for pupils;
- [ ] frequently encouraged students to set appropriate and realistic goals for themselves;

☐ spent time and effort in creating an atmosphere of concern about the importance of learning the lesson content;
☐ more often provided opportunities for learner success;
☐ more often provided immediate feedback to learners;
☐ more often checked the level of mastery being achieved (and proceeded only if an acceptable level of learning was evident);
☐ gave more appropriate consideration to the length and spacing of practice;
☐ in general provided more meaningful and coherent presentations.

(Based on McCormick: 1979, p.60 and reproduced with permission.)

# REFERENCES

Anderson, K. F. (1985) The development of spelling ability and linguistic strategies. *The Reading Teacher* 39 (2): 140-147.

Anderson, L. S. (1978) The aggressive child. *Children Today* 7 (1): 11-14.

Ashcraft, M. H. (1985) Is it far fetched that some of us remember our number facts? *Journal for Research in Mathematics Education* 16 (2): 99-105.

Asher, S. R. & Dodge, K. A. (1986) Identifying children who are rejected by their peers. *Developmental Psychology* 22 (4): 414-449.

Auten, A. (1983) Help for reluctant writers. *Language Arts* 60 (7): 921-926.

Baarda, W. (1982) The place of phonics. *Australian Journal of Reading* 5 (3): 166-167.

Baker, E. L., Herman, J. L. & Yeh, J. P. (1981) Fun and games; their contribution to basic skills instruction. *American Educational Research Journal* 18 (1): 83-92.

Beardslee, E. C. (1978) Teaching computational skills with a calculator. In Suydam, M. N. & Reys, R. E. *Developing Computational Skills*. Reston, National Council of Teachers of Mathematics.

Beattie, I. D. (1986) Modelling operations and algorithms. *Arithmetic Teacher* 33 (6): 23-28.

Bendell, D., Tollefson, N. & Fine, M. (1980) Interaction of locus of control and the performance of learning disabled adolescents. *Journal of Learning Disabilities* 13 (2): 83-86.

Bender, M., Valletutti, P. & Bender, R. (1976) *Teaching the moderately and severely handicapped. Vol. III*. Baltimore, University Park Press.

Berrill, R. (1982) The slow learner and the gifted child. In Cornelius, M. *Teaching Mathematics*. London, Croom Helm.

Bloom, S. (1978) *Peer and cross-age tutoring in the school*. Hawthorn, Australian Council for Educational Research.

Bourke, S. (1981) Community expectations of numeracy in schools. *SET Research Information for Teachers. No. 1*. Hawthorn, A.C.E.R.

Brophy, J. E. (1979) Teacher behaviour and student learning. *Educational Leadership* 37 (1): 33-38.

Broughton, R. (1975) *One-minute multiplication and division tests*. Unpublished dissertation. Adelaide, Torrens College.

Burns, M. (1986) Teaching 'what to do' in arithmetic vs. teaching 'what to do and why'. *Educational Leadership* 43 (7): 34-38.

Byrnes, D. A. (1984) Social isolates and the teacher. *Educational Forum* 48 (3): 373-381.

Canino, F. J. (1981) Learned-helplessness theory. *Journal of Special Education* 15 (4): 471-484.

Carpenter, T. P. (1985) Research on the role of structure in thinking. *Arithmetic Teacher* 32 (6): 58-60.

Cartledge, G. & Milburn, J. F. (1978) The case for teaching social skills in the classroom: a review. *Review of Educational Research* 1 (1): 133-156.

Chase, W., Lyon, D. & Ericsson, K. (1981) Individual differences in memory span. In Friedman, H., Das, J. & O'Connor, N. (eds) *Intelligence and Learning*. London, Plenum Press.

Cockcroft, W. H. (1982) *Mathematics Counts*. Report of Committee of Enquiry into the teaching of mathematics in schools. London, H.M.S.O.

Cohen, N. J. & Minde, K. (1983) The hyperactive syndrome in kindergarten children. *Journal of Child Psychology and Psychiatry* 24 (3): 443-455.

Coleman, M. C. & Gilliam, J. E. (1983) Disturbing behaviours in the classroom; a survey of teachers' attitudes. *Journal of Special Education* 17 (2): 121-129.

Copeland, R. W. (1974) *Diagnostic and learning activities in mathematics.* New York, Macmillan.

Cripps, C. (1978) *Catchwords. Ideas for teaching spelling.* Sydney, Harcourt, Brace & Javanovich.

Cripps, C. (1983) A report of an experiment to see whether young children can be taught to write from memory. *Remedial Education* 18 (1): 19-24.

Csapo, M. (1983) Effectiveness of coaching socially withdrawn and isolated children in specific social skills. *Educational Psychology* 3 (1): 31-42.

Darch, C., Carnine, D. & Gersten, R. (1984) Explicit instruction in mathematics problem solving. *Journal of Educational Research* 77 (6): 351-359.

Davis, R. B. (1984) *Learning mathematics.* London, Croom Helm.

Dixon, R. (1976) *Morphographic Spelling.* Chicago, Science Research Associates.

Eeds-Kniep, M. (1979) The frenetic fanatic phonic backlash. *Language Arts* 56 (8): 909-917.

Ehri, L. C. & Wilce, L. S. (1985) Movement into reading. Is the first stage of printed word learning visual or phonetic? *Reading Research Qtly* 20 (2): 163-179.

Engelhardt, J. M. (1982) Using computational errors in diagnostic teaching. *Arithmetic Teacher* 29 (8): 16-19.

Espiner, D., Wilton, K. & Glynn, T. (1985) Social interaction and acceptance of mildly retarded children in a mainstream setting. *Australian Journal of Special Education* 9 (2): 8-15.

Finch, M. & Hops, H. (1983) Remediation of social withdrawal in young children. In LeCroy, C. W. *Social skills training for children and youth.* New York, Haworth.

Fox, B. & Routh, D. K. (1984) Phonemic analysis and synthesis as word attack skills. *Journal of Educational Research* 76 (6): 1059-1064.

Franco, D., Christoff, K., Crimmins, D. & Kelly, J. (1983) Social skills training for an extremely shy adolescent. *Behaviour Therapy* 14: 568-575.

Fredericks, H. D. B. (1976) *The teaching research curriculum for moderately and severely handicapped.* Springfield, Thomas.

Gannon, P. (1983) Social skills training for the handicapped in mainstream classrooms. *Australian Journal of Special Education* 7 (2): 14-17.

Gersten, R. & Carnine, D. (1986) Direct instruction in reading comprehension. *Educational Leadership* 43 (7): 70-78.

Gillespie, P. H. & Johnson, L. E. (1974) *Teaching reading to the mildly retarded child.* Columbus, Merrill.

Gillet, S. & Bernard, M. E. (1985) *Reading Rescue.* Hawthorn, A.C.E.R.

Ginsburg, H. & Baroody, A. (1983) *TEMA: Test of early mathematics ability.* Austin, Pro-Ed.

Gollasch, F. V. (1982) *Language & Literacy. Selected writings of Kenneth Goodman.* London, Routledge.

Goodman, Y. M. & Burke, C. (1972) *Reading miscue inventory.* London, Collier-Macmillan.

Graves, D. H. (1981) Writing research for the eighties. *Language Arts* 58 (2): 197-206.

Graves, D. H. (1983) *Writing. Teachers and children at work.* Exeter, New Hampshire, Heinemann.

Gresham, F. M. (1982) Social skills instruction for exceptional children. *Theory into Practice* 21 (2): 129-133.

Gresham, F. M. (1984) Social skills and self-efficacy for exceptional children. *Exceptional Children* 51 (3): 253-261.

Hallahan, D. P. & Kauffman, J. M. (1986) *Exceptional Children (3rd ed).* Englewood Cliffs, Prentice-Hall.

Heddens, J. W. (1986) Bridging the gap between concrete and abstract. *Arithmetic Teacher* 33 (6): 14-17.

Hegarty, S. (1982) Integration and the comprehensive school. *Educational Review* 34 (2): 99-105.

Holdaway, D. (1982) Shared book experience: teaching reading using favourite books. *Theory into Practice* 21 (4): 293-300.

Horne, M. D. (1982) Facilitating positive peer interactions among handicapped and non-handicapped students. *Exceptional Child* 29 (2): 79-86.

Humes, A. (1983) Putting writing research into practice. *Elementary School Journal* 84 (1): 3-17.

Jackson, M. (1972) *Reading disability: experiment, innovation and individual therapy.* Sydney, Angus & Robertson.

Janke, R. W. (1980) Computational errors of mentally retarded students. *Psychology in the Schools* 17 (1): 30-32.

Johnson, R. & Johnson, D. W. (1980) The social integration of handicapped students into the mainstream. In Reynolds, M. C. (ed.)*Social Environment of the schools.* Reston, Council for Exceptional Children.

Johnson, T. & Johnson, R. (1977) The use of comics in remedial teaching. In Widlake, P. (ed.) *Remedial Education: Programmes and Progress.* London, Longman.

Jones, G., Thornton, C. & Toohey, M. (1985) A multi-option programme for learning basic addition facts. *Journal of Learning diabilities* 18 (6): 319-325.

Kemp, M. (1980) *Reading-language processes: assessment & teaching.* Adelaide, Australian Reading Association.

Kokaska, C. J. (1985) Resource teachers have problems too. *Academic Therapy* 21 (2): 189-192.

Lavers, P., Pickup, M. & Thomson, M. (1986) Factors to consider in implementing an in-class support system. *Support for Learning* 1 (3): 32-35.

Lawrence, E. A. & Winschel, J. F. (1975) Locus of control: implications for special education. *Exceptional Children* 41 (7): 483-489.

LeBlanc, J. F. (1977) You can teach problem solving. *Arithmetic Teacher* 25 (2): 16-20.

Lewis, R. B. & Doorlag, D. H. (1983) *Teaching special students in the mainstream.* Columbus, Merrill.

Lewkowicz, N. K. (1980) Phonemic awareness training: what to teach and how to teach it. *Journal of Educational Psychology* 72 (5): 686-700.

Little, T. L. (1978) The teacher-consultant model. *Journal of Special Education* 12 (3): 345-355.

Lovell, K. (1971) *The growth of understanding in mathematics.* London, Holt, Rinehart & Winston.

McCormick, W. (1979) Teachers can learn to teach more effectively. *Educational Leadership* 37 (1): 59-60.

MacDonald, T. H. (1975) Strategies in teaching mathematics to the slow learner. *Australian Journal of Remedial Education* 7 (3): 19-24.

McLeod, J. & Atkinson, J. (1972) *Domuin Phonic Workshop.* Edinburgh, Oliver & Boyd.

McNaughton, S. (1981) Low progress readers and teacher instructional behaviour. *Exceptional Child* 28 (3): 167-176.

149

Madden, N. A. & Slavin, R. E. (1983) Effects of co-operative learning on the social acceptance of mainstreamed academically handicapped students. *Journal of Special Education* 17 (2): 171-182.

Merrett, F. & Wheldall, K. (1984) Classroom behaviour problems which junior school teachers find most troublesome. *Educational Studies* 10 (2): 87-92.

Meyen, E. L., Vergason, G. A. & Whelan, R. J. (1972) *Strategies for teaching exceptional children.* Denver, Love.

Monroe, J. (1977) Language abilities and mathematics performance. *Australian Journal of Remedial Education* 9 (3): 24-31.

Montague, M. & Candace, S. (1986) The effect of cognitive strategy training on verbal math problem solving performance. *Journal of Learning Disabilities* 19 (1): 26-33.

Moyle, D. (1982) Recent developments in reading and their effects upon remedial education. *Remedial Education* 17 (4): 151-155.

Naidoo, S. (1981) Teaching methods and their rationale. In Pavlidis, G. & Miles, T. *Dyslexia research and its application to education.* Chichester, Wiley.

Neale, M. (1966) *Neale Analysis of Reading Ability.* London, Macmillan.

Nelson, D. W. (1983) Math is not a problem when you know how to visualise it. *Instructor* 93 (4): 54-55.

Newman, J. M. (1984) Language learning and computers. *Language Arts* 61 (5) 480-483.

Omanson, R. C. (1985) Knowing words and understanding texts. In Carr, T. W. *The development of reading skills.* San Francisco, Jossey-Bass.

Perrott, E. (1982) *Effective teaching.* London, Longman.

Peters, M. L. (1967) *Spelling: caught or taught?* London, Routledge.

Pinsent, P. (1984) Some current perspectives on the writing of young children. *Early Child Development and Care* 14: 125-139.

Radlauer, E. & Radlauer, R. (1974) *Bowmar Reading Incentive Program.* Glendale, Bowmar.

Raim, J. (1983) Influences of the teacher-pupil interaction on disabled readers. *Reading Teacher* 36 (8): 810-813.

Reisman, F. K. (1972) *A guide to the diagnostic teaching of arithmetic.* Columbus, Merrill.

Reynolds, M. C. (1984) Classification of students with handicaps. *Review of Research in Education* 11: 63-92.

Richards, P. (1982) Difficulties in learning mathematics. In Cornelius, M. *Teaching Mathematics.* London, Croom Helm.

Riley, J. D. & Pachtman, A. (1978) Reading mathematical word problems. *Journal of Reading* 21 (6): 531-534.

Rogers, H. & Saklofske, D. H. (1985) Self-concept, locus of control and performance expectations of learning disabled children. *Journal of Learning Disabilities* 18 (5): 273-278.

Roseman, L. (1985) Ten essential concepts for remediation in mathematics. *Mathematics Teacher* 78 (7): 502-507.

Salend, S. J. (1984) Factors contributing to the development of successful mainstreaming programs. *Exceptional Children* 50 (5): 409-416.

Sayers, B. J. (1983) Aboriginal mathematical concepts: a cultural & linguistic explanation for some of the problems. *The Aboriginal Child at School* 11 (1): 3-18.

Searle, D. (1984) Scaffolding: who's building whose building? *Language Arts* 61 (5): 480-483.

Sears, H. C. & Johnson, D. M. (1986) The effects of visual imagery on spelling performance. *Journal of Educational Research* 79 (4): 230-233.

Sewell, G. (1982) *Reshaping remedial education*. London, Croom Helm.

Sindelar, P. & Deno, S. L. (1978) The effectiveness of resource programming. *Journal of Special Education* 12 (1): 17-28.

Sippola, A. E. (1985) What to teach for reading readiness. *Reading Teacher* 39 (2): 162-167.

Skemp, R. (1976) Relational understanding and instrumental understanding. *Mathematics Teaching* 77: 20-26.

Slade, D. L. (1986) Developing foundations for organisational skills. *Academic Therapy* 21 (3): 261-266.

Smith, C. A. (1982) *Promoting the social development of young children* Palo Alto, Mayfield.

Smith, F. (1978) *Understanding Reading*. New York, Holt, Rinehart & Winston.

Smith, N. B. (1969) The many faces of reading comprehension. *Reading Teacher* 23 (3): 249-259.

Sowder, L., Moyer, M. & Moyer, J. (1986) Diagnosing a student's understanding of operations. *Arithmetic Teacher* 33 (9): 22-25.

Stobart, G. (1986) Is integrating the handicapped psychologically defensible? *Bulletin of the British Psychological Society* 39: 1-3.

Stott, D. H. (1962) *Programmed Reading Kit*. Edinburgh, Holmes McDougall.

Stott, D. H. (1981) Teaching reading; the psycholinguistic invasion. *Reading* 15 (3): 19-25.

Suydam, M. N. (1986) Manipulative materials and achievement. *Arithmetic Teacher* 33 (6): 10-32.

Telford, C. W. & Sawrey, J. M. (1981) *The Exceptional Individual (4th ed)* Englewood Cliffs, Prentice-Hall.

Thomas, D. (1986) Special educational needs: translating policies into practice. *Journal of Curriculum Studies* 18 (1): 100-101.

Thompson, R., White, K. & Morgan, D. (1982) Teacher-student interaction patterns in classrooms with mainstreamed mildly handicapped students. *American Educational Research Journal* 19 (2): 220-236.

Thornton, C. A. & Wilmot, B. (1986) Special learners. *Arithmetic Teacher* 33 (6): 38-41.

Treiman, R. (1985) Phonemic analysis, spelling and reading. In Carr, T. H. (ed.) *The development of reading skills*. San Francisco, Jossey-Bass.

Turnbull, A. P. & Schulz, J. B. (1979) *Mainstreaming handicapped students*. Boston, Allyn & Bacon.

Turner, T. & Alston, J. (1986) Teacher-talk and pupil comprehension in special needs primary pupils. *Support for Learning* 1 (3). 8-12.

Underhill, R. G., Uprichard, A. E. & Heddens, J. W. (1980) *Diagnosing mathematical difficulties*. Columbus, Merrill.

Walden, T. A. & Ramey, C. T. (1983) Locus of control and academic achievement. *Journal of Educational Psychology* 75 (3): 347-358.

Wang, M. C. (1981) Mainstreaming exceptional children: some instructional design and implementation considerations. *Elementary School Journal* 81 (4): 195-221.

Wang, M C. & Birch, J. W. (1984) Effective special education in regular classes. *Exceptional Children* 50 (5): 391-398.

Wang, M. C. & Lindvall, C. M. (1984) Individual differences and school learning environments. *Review of Research in Education* 11: 161-225.

151

Wang, M. C. & Stiles, B. (1976) An investigation of children's concept of self-responsibility for their school learning. *American Educational Research Journal* 13 (3): 159-179.

Wang, M. C. & Walberg, H. J. (1985) *Adapting instruction to individual differences.* Berkeley, McCutchan for N.S.S.E.

Wendon, L. (1983) Researcher's challenge. *Reading* 17 (1): 55-60.

Westwood, P. S. (1975) *The remedial teacher's handbook.* Edinburgh, Oliver & Boyd.

Westwood, P. S. (1982) Strategies for improving social interaction of handicapped children in regular classes. *Australian Journal of Remedial Education* 14 (4): 23-24.

Westwood, P. S. (1984) Asking the crucial question: 'Is integration working for this child?' *Australian Journal of Remedial Education* 16 (1): 10-12.

Westwood, P. S. (1985) When writing is a problem. *Australian Journal of Remedial Education* 17 (1): 23-24.

Westwood, P. S. (1986) Contemporary views on the teaching of reading. *Australian Journal of Remedial Education* 18 (2): 9-13.

Westwood, P. S., Harris-Hughes, M., Lucas, G., Nolan, J. & Scrymgeour, K. (1974) One-minute tests of addition and subtraction facts. *Remedial Education* 9 (2): 70-72.

Widlake, P. (1983) *How to reach the hard to teach.* Milton Keynes, Open University Press.

Williams, J. P. (1980) Teaching decoding with an emphasis on phoneme analysis and phoneme blending. *Journal of Educational Psychology* 72 (1): 1-15.

Williams, R. (1986) Top ten principles for teaching reading. *English Language Teaching Journal* (ELT) 40 (1): 42-45.

Wooster, A. (1986) Social skills training and reading gains. *Educational Research* 28 (1): 68-71.

Yule, V. (1986) A complement to Bullock: the American report 'Becoming a nation of readers'. *Reading* 20 (2): 82-88.

# GENERAL INDEX